JUMPING

JUMPING

MALCOLM ARNOLD
British Amateur Athletic Board

THE CROWOOD PRESS

First published in 1986 by
THE CROWOOD PRESS
Crowood House, Ramsbury
Marlborough, Wiltshire SN8 2HE

British Library Cataloguing in Publication Data

Arnold, Malcolm,
  Jumping.
  1. Jumping
  I. Title
  796.4'32   GV1075

  ISBN 0–946284–82–2

Acknowledgements

To my wife Madelyn for her help and encouragement; to Howard
Payne for Figs 15 to 26, 47 to 59 and 72 to 79; to Helmar Hommel for
Figs 65 to 70; and to Stan Greenberg for supplying the statistics in
the appendix.

Line illustrations by Annette Findlay

Series Adviser David Bunker, Lecturer, University of Loughborough

Cover photographs courtesy of Mark Shearman

Typeset by Lee Editorial/Volant Art Services
Printed in Great Britain

Contents

Malcolm Arnold qualified as a teacher of physical education at Loughborough College in 1961. Since then, he has been deeply involved in track and field athletics. As a competitive athlete, he was ranked fourth in Britain in 1962 in the triple jump, and represented the Amateur Athletic Association on a number of occasions. In 1968 he was appointed Director of Coaching in Uganda, East Africa, where he coached a number of world class athletes, including John Akii-Bua, the 1972 Olympic Champion and world record holder 1972–1976 in the 400 metres hurdles. He was appointed BAAB National Coach for Wales in 1974 and has subsequently coached many jumpers in the Great Britain team. He has been Chief Coach for sprinting and hurdling and is currently Chief Coach for the jumping events.

The jumping events in athletics provide a stimulating challenge to both beginners and experienced athletes. To strike the take-off board at top speed in the long jump or triple jump and then to control the flight and landing is a very satisfying feeling. The pole vault and high jump present different but equally exciting challenges, when a well-executed take-off is rewarded with a successful bar clearance.

I am honoured to give a foreword to this excellent publication by my friend and colleague, Malcolm Arnold. Both as an athlete and now as Chief Coach for jumping and pole vaulting within the National Coaching and Performance Plan, Malcolm has committed much time and energy to the study of these events. The depth of that study, the thoroughness of his coaching methodology, and his immense experience of working with athletes brings real vitality to this outstanding text. The reader, whether a competitor, teacher or coach, will be left much the wiser from its content. I believe that these pages will lead to far more effective work in the jumping events in the years to come.

Malcolm Arnold, as a successful former triple jumper himself and now a National Athletics Coach, provides just this kind of advice which will help you in your event. The jumping events are fun and just as enjoyable when you work hard to get things right. A little thought and a lot of practice will work wonders and quickly improve your heights and distances.

The advice and coaching hints given in this book are invaluable and will help you to 'get it right' and set you on your way to success. Good luck in your endeavours! I hope you have as much enjoyment and satisfaction in your career as I have had in mine.

This publication will ensure that your learning in the jumping disciplines has a perfect take-off!

Frank W. Dick
Director of Coaching
British Amateur Athletic Board

Lynn Davies, MBE
Olympic long jump champion 1964 and
British record holder for the long jump

1   History

Who can say with any degree of certainty how the jumps we know today as the pole vault, high jump, long jump and triple jump originated? Observe young people at play and you will see that any form of jumping for distance or height – up or down – is a natural, untaught human play activity. As athletics became formalised in the nineteenth and twentieth centuries, jumping events became an important part of athletics competitions. During the years the events have developed, some with their own sophisticated equipment, into the spectacular activities practised by athletes at both the grass roots and elite levels of athletics today.

POLE VAULTING

Pole vaulting as we now know it is far removed from its roots. There are drawings of men vaulting onto a horse with the aid of a pole in ancient Greek times, although there is no reference to pole vaulting in the ancient Greek Olympics. The father of early pole vaulting is regarded as J. C. F. Gutsmuths, the German whose book *Gymnastic fur die Jugend* mentioned 'the leap in length, with and without a pole'. Professor Voelker, a German exiled in England, founded the London Gymnastic Society in 1826. Apparently it was this society that was responsible for the spread of pole leaping techniques.

There are records of pole vaulting in the Lake District of England in the late 1830s.

In the 1840s and 1850s vaulters recorded heights of eight and nine feet (2.4 and 2.7m). Later, in 1876 Edwin Woodburn cleared eleven feet (3.4m) for the first time and in 1887 Tom Ray cleared eleven feet six inches (3.5m).

Historically, pole vaulting has always had its controversies. The first occurred when the vaulters of the Lake District developed a 'swarming' or 'pole climbing' technique, whereby the vaulter planted the pole, swung it to the upright position and then climbed hand over hand before levering himself over the bar. This technique was very controversial and was eventually banished. National records for the pole climbing techniques existed from 1866 until 1891 (*see* appendix) when today's more conventional technique was recognised. Reference to the banning of the 'swarming' technique is still made in the rules today. The Amateur Athletic Association's rule 81(h) iii says: 'A competitor fails if he, at the moment he makes a vault, or after leaving the ground, places his lower hand above the upper one or moves his upper hand higher up the pole'. With the banning of this technique, supremacy in pole vaulting passed to the USA where it remained for a very long time, until the more recent ascendence of the French, Polish and USSR vaulters.

The development of equipment for pole vaulting is a further area of interest. Today's high technology vaulting poles have led to the vaulters of the 1980s clearing the six metre barrier. Nineteenth-century vaulters used heavy ash poles with spikes in the end. They took off from grass runways without a planting box and landed on grass on the other side of the bar! Bamboo poles proved to be much lighter and slightly flexible, but did not really become popular until after the 1900 Olympics. The bamboo pole era was at its peak in the 1930s and continued until 1948. An aluminium pole was introduced in the 1930s, but the tapered steel pole, introduced in about 1946 from Sweden, proved more successful. These poles were used until the late 1950s. The first glass-reinforced plastic poles were introduced in 1948, but it was not until the late 1950s that they became lighter and more flexible. Since their introduction, technology has improved their quality and reliability to a very high level.

Fibreglass poles have also been a centre of controversy on a number of occasions since their introduction. In a personal conversation in 1976 with Harold Abrahams (the 1924 Olympic 100m gold medallist and the man in the IAAF responsible for changes in technical rules at that time), he suggested that the IAAF should have banned the fibreglass pole, and were slow not to do so, on the grounds of unorthodoxy. Today's successful pole vaulter uses the fibreglass pole exclusively. The high price of the best poles, manufactured in the USA, prevents the event becoming universally popular.

As vaulters have jumped higher, so the landing areas have had to be improved to prevent serious injury. Today's landing areas are large, soft to land on and very expensive. Only the foolhardy will encourage or engage in vaulting on an unsuitable area. There are minimum sizes and densities for landing areas and these must be strictly observed.

HIGH JUMP

The high jump is another event that has benefited from the development of soft, raised landing areas. They have allowed developments in technique which otherwise would have been impossible. In the nineteenth century, like pole vaulters, high jumpers took off from grass and landed on grass. Their technique was dominated by a regard for their own safety. The scissors technique developed, where the athletes could see the landing area at all times through the jump. As the athletes became more adventurous, they employed a back layout scissors technique to give a more efficient bar clearance position. They crossed the bar on their back and landed in a more precarious position. Landing areas 'developed' with piles of sand placed to provide a little more safety. With more

Fig 1 Scissors high jump.

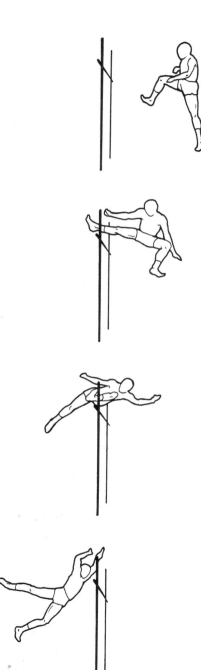

adventurous back layout techniques, broken wrists and arms became more commonplace.

The Eastern cut-off was a popular if complicated style of jumping until the 1940s, when the 'roll' techniques gained superiority. The western roll was the first popular roll technique and dominated the scene until the mid 1950s. From 1956 the straddle gained superiority until an

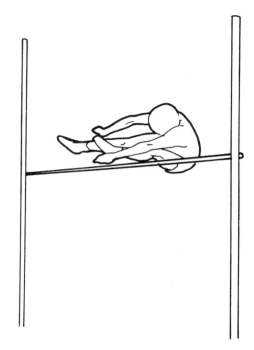

Fig 3   Western roll high jump.

Fig 2   Eastern cut-off high jump.

amazing development took place in the Mexico City Olympic Games of 1968. Dick Fosbury of the USA used a different back layout technique, which was subsequently called the Fosbury flop. This technique needs a good, safe landing area and must not be attempted without one. Fosbury's technique demanded that the athlete

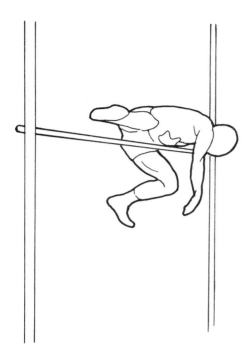

Fig 4   Straddle high jump.

should take off from the foot furthest from the bar and cross the bar with the back arched. This technique is simpler than most others, is easy to learn and has led to jumpers clearing greater heights all over the world. The reasons for these particular developments in high jump technique over the years are explained more fully in Chapter 4.

LONG JUMP

The long jump has its roots in the ancient Games of Greece, but not in the form we know today. Today's event is a running long jump, but the ancient Greek form was a standing long jump. The jumpers used weights or 'halteres'. As the jumper took off he swung the weights forwards, so that in mid-air his arms and legs were almost parallel. Before landing he swung the weights backwards and released them, a movement which shot the legs forwards and thus lengthened the jump. The

Fig 5   The Fosbury flop.

Fig 6   This technique needs a good, safe landing area.

jumping weights were hand-held and weighed anything between two and ten pounds (0.9 and 4.5kg). This technique influenced the flight path of the jumper's centre of gravity and enabled him to jump further. The jumpers took off from the 'threshold' and landed in a dug-up area called the 'skamma'. To 'jump beyond the skamma' was the expression for an extraordinary feat. The current AAA rule book tells us that the use of weights or grips is forbidden. This rule has its origins in the eighteenth century, when British jumpers also used 'halteres' to increase their natural jumping distance.

Professional jumpers in the nineteenth century used all sorts of tricks, from jumping weights to elevated jumping ramps. One story tells us that 'J. Howard of Chester jumped 29 feet 7 inches (9.02m) in 1854'! It was said that the use of jumping weights 'added at least 8 feet (2.4m) to his jump'. No doubt an elevated take-off ramp was also used.

Olympic long jumping is full of great performances, particularly those of Jesse Owens, Bob Beamon and Carl Lewis. The American men have won seventeen out of the twenty Olympic long jump contests, the series being interrupted by Petterson of Sweden in 1920 and Britain's Lynn Davies in 1964. The Americans did not compete in the 1980 Olympic Games in Moscow.

Jesse Owens set a world record of 8.13m in 1935, which remained unbeaten for twenty-five years. In 1968, in the Olympic Games in Mexico City, Bob Beamon became the first to jump beyond 28 feet and 29 feet (8.5 and 8.8m) when he cleared 29 feet 2½ inches (8.90m). To date this record has not been beaten, although Carl Lewis is threatening that mark.

Ladies' long jumping has witnessed significant improvements in recent years, with the Soviets, Rumanians and East Germans in the lead. Vilma Bardauskiene (USSR) beat the 7m barrier for the first time in 1978 in the European Championships in Prague, Czechoslovakia. Since then the world record has fallen to athletes who are excellent sprinters and strong jumpers but not particularly good technicians.

TRIPLE JUMP

The triple jump is also thought to have been contested in the ancient Olympic Games. A jump of 16.76m was reported by Phaylus, an outstanding Greek athlete. This statistic is hard to accept as one for long jumping and it must have been achieved with some type of multiple jump. We shall never know the exact version of the jump, but it could have been an early version of the triple jump. The documented history of the triple jump really begins in the late eighteenth century, although it is accepted that athletes triple jumped before this date. There has been some change in technique over the years. It is known that jumpers preferred to use their stronger leg twice in contests in the nineteenth and early twentieth centuries, with a hop–hop–jump technique. A rule change required the change to the present day hop–step–jump technique.

The triple jump has also produced some outstanding characters in the history of the event. Perhaps the most famous is the durable and brilliant athlete from the USSR, Victor Saneyev. He was the Olympic champion in 1968, 1972 and 1976 and the silver medallist in 1980, a feat which is unlikely to be repeated in any event.

Dominance by certain nations has also

been a notable feature in the development of the triple jump over the last sixty years. Japanese dominance began in 1928 and lasted for the next two Olympic Games. Mikio Oda won in 1928 with 15.21m. Chuhei Nambu won in 1932 with a world record 15.72m and Naota Tajima won with another world record of 16.00m in the Berlin Games of 1936.

Brazilian dominance began in 1952 when Adhemar da Silva set two world records in the same Olympic competition in Helsinki. He also won the 1956 Olympic triple jump in Melbourne, Australia. Poland has produced famous triple jumpers too, Josef Schmidt being a technical trend-setter and Olympic champion in 1960 in Rome and 1964 in Tokyo. More recently Zsislaw Hoffman won the first world championships in 1983 in Helsinki, Finland.

Victor Saneyev has been mentioned in particular, yet he is only one of many outstanding Soviet jumpers over the last thirty-five years. The USSR has always produced triple jumpers of the highest standard with almost monotonous regularity. In recent years they have been the most dominant nation.

Perhaps the most brilliant jumper of recent times was Joao de Oliveira from Brazil, who set a world record 17.89m at altitude in Mexico City in 1975. Unfortunately de Oliveira suffered crippling injuries in a car crash, which ended his career.

Altitude performances in all the jumping events have often raised the question of their legality. This is because the rarified air and the reduced pull of gravity inevitably assists the power/speed events like the jumps. Some argue that records should be disallowed over a certain altitude, just as records are disallowed in sprinting events when the following wind is over the two metres per second limit.

2 Fundamentals

ANALYSIS

All jumping events have a common pattern. Analysis reveals that each event consists of the following parts:

1. *An approach run*, in which optimum speed (high jump) or maximum controlled speed (pole vault, long jump and triple jump) is required.
2. *A take-off*, in which each event has its own specialised requirements.
3. *A flight* though the air, in which each event also has its own specialised requirements.
4. *A landing*, where each event requires either technical efficiency to gain maximum distance (long and triple jump), or safety in landing from a great height (pole vault and high jump).

So that these four fundamental aspects of jumping can be plainly understood, they will be discussed in general terms now. The specifics of each event will be discussed in more detail in following chapters.

Approach Run *(Fig 7)*

There are three vital aspects to the approach run: a combination of speed and rhythm; correct postural adjustment during the run; and accuracy at the take-off point. Each must be understood, learned, practised and perfected.

There are very few athletes in the world born with the talent of Jesse Owens or Carl Lewis. Those of a lesser talent should very quickly understand that a mastery of fundamentals can improve performance significantly. Correct application of fundamentals can really improve technique and distances jumped.

Speed and Rhythm

In the pole vault, triple jump and long jump maximum controlled speed in the final strides before take-off is imperative. In recent studies conducted in the European Championships in Athens in 1982 and in the World Championships in Helsinki in 1983, it was shown that an increase in run-up speed by the world's best jumpers led to an improvement in performance.

In the triple jump, in the last three strides before take-off, run-up speeds between 10m and 10.5m per second were recorded. In the men's long jump in the same world championships the approach speed of the winner, Carl Lewis (USA), exceeded 11m per second and that of the ladies' winner, world record holder Heike Drechsler (GDR), exceeded 10m per second. Of the other performers in the men's event, speeds between 10m and 10.5m per second were common as were speeds between 9.5m and 10m per second in the ladies' event.

In the pole vault, where the vaulter has to deal with the difficulties of sprinting and carrying his pole, very high run-up speeds between 9.2m to 9.6m per second were also registered in the final three strides before take-off.

Fundamentals

In a world where jumping performance improvement is accelerating, run-up speed is a vital component of that improvement. Fast sprinters are dominating the jumping events. Those athletes who are slow on the runway must work very hard to eliminate any speed deficiency.

In the high jump an optimum speed of approach is required, that is the correct speed for the strength and ability of the athlete in question. The speed of approach has a positive influence on lift at take-off. An increase in speed will give better contraction in the muscles of the take-off leg. In turn this develops maximum tension in the muscles and a greater reaction between the take-off foot and the jumping surface. The end result of this process is good vertical lift, the quality a high jumper is always searching for. If the athlete approaches at too high a speed, the take-off leg could collapse. If the approach is too slow, then the reaction of the leg muscles may be reduced and the vertical lift will be lost. Through assessment of an athlete's physical capabilities, the most appropriate take-off speed can be worked out. Gold medallist Dick Fosbury's approach speed in the 1968 Olympic Games was estimated at 8m per second, and approach speeds in excess of 7m per second are regularly recorded for top jumpers. Essentially, the stronger the athlete, the higher is the approach speed that can be employed.

Rhythm in the approach run relates to the application of speed in the right place. So often young athletes are seen to reach top speed (or optimum speed in the high jump) too soon before take-off. This leads to an unsuccessful jump. When practising the approach run, great value is attached to rhythm runs as well as accuracy runs.

By practising the rhythm of the run, athlete and coach can ensure the application of speed at the correct place in the approach. In competition, rhythm runs must always be undertaken before the accuracy runs. It is only the accuracy run that reflects the correct postural adjustments before and through take-off. The exact nature of rhythm runs and accuracy runs are explained in the chapter on training.

Postural adjustment through the approach run must be understood, so that the athlete arrives at the take-off point with the correct body position. Very late postural adjustments will lead to a poor take-off position and a poor jump. *Fig 7* illustrates the postural changes throughout the approach run of a long jumper or triple jumper (and, with slight adaptation, that of a pole vaulter too). Essentially, an athlete begins running by leaning forward. As he picks up speed he runs in a more upright position, and as he approaches take-off his hips sink in readiness for the upward spring. In practical terms, the hip sink should not be over-emphasised for it will happen naturally. If this point is over-emphasised, then the hips may sink too deeply into a position from which the athlete may not recover. Postural adjustment is an important part of the jumper's training and must be included in practice for the approach run and take-off.

Accuracy of take-off position is obviously necessary and it should be considered together with postural changes, speed and rhythm on the runway. In the long jump and triple jump, an athlete's effort is measured from the scratch line. If he takes off beyond that line it is a no jump and if he takes off behind that line he loses distance.

Similarly, the high jumper takes off from a particular point, so that the highest point

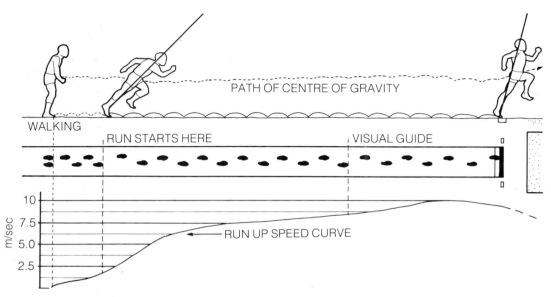

PATH OF CENTRE OF GRAVITY

WALKING

RUN STARTS HERE

VISUAL GUIDE

RUN UP SPEED CURVE

m/sec

10
7.5
5.0
2.5

Fig 7   Approach run characteristics.

of his flight occurs exactly over the lowest point of the bar. The pole vaulter must also ensure that his take-off foot is placed directly underneath his top hand at take-off. Without this, smooth transference of the athlete to the pole is difficult.

The athlete approaches the take-off point from anything between twenty and forty metres away. To place the foot precisely on one particular spot on the runway is a difficult skill. Jumping begins on the runway, so the mastery of runway skills is vital.

Take-off

The approach run and take-off phases appear under separate headings, but they are not really separate. In an ideal jump each phase complements the other.

As posture alters, the running strides develop into a pattern over the final part of the approach run. In a good jump, the hips sink on the penultimate stride and this stride lengthens slightly. Thereafter, the final stride can shorten from between six and twenty-two centimetres. Recent research into the high jump has suggested that the penultimate stride should be about thirty centimetres longer than the last stride. This is why when an athlete practises his approach run for competition, he should actually take off, rather than just run through without taking off. This helps achieve absolute accuracy. If the athlete does not take off during a rehearsal run for competition, then the final adjustments over the last two strides are not accurately reflected. An inaccurate approach will result.

The angle of take-off (that is the angle the path of the centre of gravity makes with the horizontal) differs for each of the horizontal jumps. The long jumper has the

Fundamentals

greatest need for height as he leaves the board. In the high jump maximum vertical lift is required and the athlete strives to get up and above the bar during flight. In the triple jump the athlete has different aims at take-off, because after the initial take-off he then has to land and take off twice more before the final landing in the pit. Consequently the triple jumper's aim is to conserve speed throughout the three phases and his take-off is much flatter than that of the long jumper. The pole vault take-off is a very specialised affair, because of the vaulter's reliance on the pole to project him into the air. Correct positioning of the body at take-off and correct timing of the plant of the pole into the box is vital.

There are many similarities in the final take-off position in all jumping events. The high jump, long jump, triple jump and pole vault show the following similarities.

1. Foot plant, where the heel of the foot lands first, but the athlete's sensation is one of a flat foot plant.
2. Vigorous extension of the contact leg at take-off to give good lift.
3. Active use of the free leg in an upward, driving action. This knee must also be worked vigorously until it is opposite the hip.
4. A stable, flat back.
5. Active use of the arms in phase with the legs (except of course in the pole vault where the arms are attached to the pole). Sometimes, in triple jump and high jump, the athlete moves one arm out of phase into a double arm shift to effect a more efficient take-off.
6. A steady, erect position of the head.

Flight

Body position and the athlete's ability to alter it during flight is important in all four jumping events. Once an athlete takes off and ceases to have contact with the ground, little will influence the flight path of his centre of gravity. However, he can change the shape of his body to give an efficient bar clearance technique in the pole vault and high jump or a better final landing position (and thus greater distance) in the long jump and triple jump. The high jump has probably seen most technical change over the years. The reason for this change has been the search for a more efficient bar clearance. Any individual high jumper has the ability to raise his centre of gravity a certain amount. Everything else being equal, he will clear the greatest height by using the most efficient bar clearance technique. This is why jumpers nowadays use the Fosbury flop, rather than the scissors technique.

In the triple jump, complex leg movements whilst the athlete is airborne serve to enable good landing positions for ensuing phases. To strike the ground with the correct foot action is important to triple jumping, and correct body position in the air before each landing ensures this. At the take-off in long jump a checking takes place, which creates a rotation about the centre of gravity. In practical terms this means that a long jumper will pitch forwards in mid-air and land awkwardly with his feet underneath his trunk. In keeping a longer body position during certain parts of the long jump, by employing a hitch kick or a hang technique, the athlete can get a good 'leg shoot' on landing and thus gain extra distance for the same expenditure of effort.

Pole vaulting, because of the influence of the pole itself, is a special case for study, but similar biomechanical laws apply. Once the athlete leaves the pole to clear the bar his flight path of centre of gravity is determined, but as in high jumping the ability to change body shape as the bar is crossed is a vital skill.

Landing

In the long and triple jump landings, the athlete must strive for an efficient position to give maximum jumping distance. Poor jumpers land in a standing position, with the feet under the trunk. Good jumpers are able to get their feet out in front of the body. If the feet are too far in front of the body the athlete will sit back into the sand and lose distance, so a compromise must be reached where the feet are as far forwards as possible without the athlete falling back into the sand. Some athletes actually do a 'skid through' landing, where the feet are held as far forwards as possible. When the feet strike the sand, the knees are collapsed and the athlete arches his back. In a good landing this technique can gain extra distance, but it is for experienced jumpers only.

In the pole vault and high jump a safe landing is necessary. Pole vault technique must give the athlete maximum penetration into the pit and the vaulter must also learn to land efficiently, by presenting as much surface area of his body to the pit as possible.

The high jumper must take off at the correct point. If he takes off too far along the bar, he stands a good chance of missing the landing area! The best take-off point lies close to the nearest upright.

3 The Pole Vault

The chapter outlining jumping history described the development of the pole vault. Pole construction technology, together with landing area development has changed the nature of the event so much from its origins, that the vaulters of the last century would have great difficulty in recognising the event today! Such is the change that present day vaulters must think of beginning on the fibreglass pole, by joining an already established coaching group at one of the centres of pole vaulting that exist. The days of the metal pole have gone, although these poles can be used for early learning activities.

LEARNING TO POLE VAULT

The initial aims in learning to vault are:

1. To gain confidence in supporting one's own body weight when swinging on a pole in various modes, such as swinging for distance, swinging down from heights or swinging on gymnasium ropes.
2. To become braver when swinging on a pole.

This initial activity can be learned using old metal poles, sturdy wooden poles, or indeed anything that will easily hold a person's body weight. The other facilities required are a firm, non-slip surface, such as dry grass, and then a long jump or triple jump runway with a well-dug sand pit.

Stance and Grip (Figs 8 to 12)

To begin with, the stance and the grip should be learned. Put the pole upright and stand behind it. Right-handers should put their right hand just above head height on the pole, with the thumb and forefinger at the top. The left hand should be opposite the chest, also with the thumb and forefinger at the top. Then, support the body weight on the pole and swing past the pole on the right side, landing again safely on the ground after a short flight. If confidence is high, keep the hands the same distance apart, but move them higher on the pole so that the right hand is at full stretch. To go one step further, put the pole in the planted position and run over seven or nine strides, plant the pole in the sand pit and take off. Confidence and enjoyment in swinging on a pole are now the aims.

First Vault (Fig 13)

After these introductory activities, more formal instruction in pole vaulting can begin. Assume the original position. Right-handers, still gripping the pole, pick it up and move the right hand opposite the right hip pocket. The left hand is held just below chest height. The hips and shoulders should be square to the front to enable the vaulter to run fast. Left-handers do vault very successfully and they should reverse the instructions given for right-handers in this book. The next target is to run, plant the pole on a firm spot on the ground and

Fig 8   The pole vaulting grip, with the right hand just above head height and the left hand opposite the chest.

Fig 9   Support your body weight on the pole.

Fig 10   Take off from your left foot.

Fig 11   Swing past the right-hand side of the pole.

The Pole Vault

Fig 12 Land safely in a controlled way.
facing forwards.

take off for a short flight (*Fig 13*). The landing must be made in a controlled way, facing forwards. Never be afraid to adjust the height of the grip on the pole. The higher the grip, the longer the flight. However, if the grip is too high the athlete stands a chance of not taking off because of insufficient momentum. Unhappy, painful landings can result from too high a hand hold. Once confidence is gained, progress can then be made towards a stable technique. These points will be helpful in gaining that stability:

1. If you are right-handed, swing past the right-hand side of the pole.
2. Take off from the left foot.
3. When planting the pole ready for taking off, stretch as high as possible with the right hand to get the pole as near to vertical as possible.

Fig 13 A beginner's first vault – run, plant the pole on a firm spot and take off for a
short flight.

Fig 14   Note the flat back, high hips and free thigh driving upwards and forwards.

Once these points have been learned, the budding pole vaulter should have confidence in supporting his own body weight. The next step is to vault for height in the conventional manner.

Plant

When beginning to vault over a bar there can be problems of co-ordination. The athlete must run fast, plant the pole into the take-off box and then take off, all in the space of a very short time. This requires the athlete to be very accurate in his actions within a very short period of time. The plant takes place over the last three strides before take-off. Initially, to help with the accuracy problem, set up high jump stands across the long jump pit with an elastic bar at a low height and allow the vaulter to plant the pole tip in the sand. This means that the athlete can plant the

pole anywhere instead of in the limited area of the planting box. Ideally the athlete should now be working on a fibreglass pole.

The timing of the plant must be solved. Think of it taking place over the final three strides into take-off. During the third stride from take-off, the bottom end of the pole begins to drop from eye-level into the box. On the penultimate contact of the left foot, the right hand begins to move from the right hip pocket to as high as possible overhead. As the right foot contacts the runway for the last time the hands and arms should be nearly in position ready for take-off. This constitutes an early plant, which is a pole vaulting essential. Without this early plant it is impossible for the vault to proceed successfully. Then, as the left foot contacts the runway for the final time before take-off, it should be directly under the top hand, with the back flat, hips high and the free thigh driven upwards and forwards into take-off (this sequence is shown in *Fig 13*).

Approach Run

The next step is to co-ordinate the approach run and the plant into the take-off. The novice vaulter is still not yet trying to bend the pole.

Here, I would like to emphasise the importance of the approach run. Some observers think that vaulting begins as the athlete leaves the ground to clear the bar. It must be understood that vaulting begins at the start of the approach run. All other things being equal, the faster a vaulter runs, the higher he will vault.

The length of the approach run varies according to age and sprinting speed. As a general rule, think of using an odd number of strides and matching the number of strides taken to the age of the athlete. The following table will help to determine the length of the approach run:

11 to 13 years – 13 strides
13 to 15 years – 15 strides
15 to 17 years – 17 strides
Mature juniors and seniors – up to 21 strides.

It is unusual for athletes to run further than twenty-one strides in their approach run. As a general rule, the faster the athlete is, the longer his approach run will be.

When learning an approach run, set it up on the track away from the landing area. If it is learned on the runway with the landing area in place, then the athlete slows down at the end of the approach, rather than speeds up. Use a planting target on a single lane on the track or the long jump runway to simulate the proper planting box.

The plan is to run with the pole the selected number of strides, say fifteen. For a right-handed vaulter, the first step will be with the left foot and the fifteenth step will be the take-off point. The aim is then to build a rhythm into the run. Achieve an optimum speed over the first ten strides; in the last five strides aim for leg speed, runnning tall with high hips, and attack into take-off.

The plant, which must be early, should be co-ordinated into the last three strides to achieve correct take-off posture. The run can be adjusted for accuracy *after* the ryhthm has been learned. Then, to achieve accuracy, relate the position of the left foot to the top (right) hand at the moment of take-off. As a rough and ready measure during training, stick some tape on the pole vault runway at the point of take-off which is directly under the top hand. If, during practice, the foot falls behind the tape, the start of the run should be moved closer. If the foot falls in front of the tape, the start of the run should be moved further away. Final accuracy must always be checked with a full take-off into a vault.

Bending the Pole *(Figs 15 to 26)*

Once the approach, plant and take-off have been learned then attempts to vault properly by bending the pole should commence.

The idea of having a flexible pole that bends substantially is to store energy in it, so that it can be used at a later stage in the vault. Thus during the take-off and the swing the athlete is concerned with putting energy into the pole. During the 'rock back' the athlete is concerned with maintaining energy in the pole – 'holding station' – and getting a good body position, so that when energy is released

Fig 15 Wladyslaw Kozakiewicz (Olympic Champion 1980) is running fast, keeping his hips and shoulders square to the front.

Fig 16 He has moved his right hand from hip level to the high position in preparation for take-off.

Fig 17 An early plant of the pole, with the take-off foot directly under the top hand.

Fig 18   A good action of the right leg, driving vigorously upwards and forwards.

Fig 19   The swing begins – the initial bend in the pole having been achieved by
         an active take-off with the correct posture.

Fig 20 Hang long, with a good distance between the top hand and the left foot.

Fig 21 As the rock back commences, lift the hips into position.

Fig 22 Aim to get the left toes to the top of the pole.

25

The Pole Vault

Fig 23 Maintain position on the pole, trying to pull along the long axis of the pole without turning too early.

Fig 24 When the pull on the pole ceases, the push begins, to achieve maximum distance between the top hand and the body's centre of gravity as it passes over the bar.

Fig 25 Kozakiewicz assumes a 'piked' position crossing the bar.

Fig 26 *He then assumes an arched 'fly-away' position. If this is assumed too early, the chest will probably push down on the bar and remove it.*

back from the pole the athlete is projected in the correct direction over the bar. Thus it is obvious that practice to gain precise co-ordination is very necessary.

The ideal point from which to begin is one where the athlete has learned to co-ordinate the approach run and take-off into a simple vault (*Fig 14*). The action of bending a fibreglass pole is so dependent upon the approach run and take-off that they must be learned first. When the process of learning to bend the pole begins, the following points should be emphasised.

During the Plant

1. Plant early. If the top hand is in position late, the vault will be a poor one.
2. Place the arms in the correct position. The top arm should not be held rigidly and should be ready to absorb the force at

take-off. Do not pull down on the pole with the top arm. Similarly, the left arm should not be so rigid that it drives the athlete away from the pole, nor should it be so soft that it allows the vaulter's chest to hit the pole. The left arm should be sufficiently braced to absorb the take-off forces and to prevent the chest from going forwards into the pole.

During Take-off

1. Achieve the correct posture (*Fig 18*).
2. Think of the take-off as an upward/forward spring.
3. Place the free thigh into the correct position (*Fig 18*).

During the Swing

1. Maintain the free thigh position.
2. Hang 'long' with as much distance as

possible between the right hand and the left foot.

3. When the rock back begins, think of swinging the left foot to the top of the pole.

During the Rock Back

The rock back begins when the pole reaches its maximum bend. Assume a good position on the pole by lifting the hips into the rock back position. When energy is released from the pole, the athlete must be in position to make best use of it. A poor position will mean a misdirected drive off the end of the pole. Try to get the knees and lower legs behind an imaginary straight line joining the ends of the pole.

Adherence to these few points will help to bend the pole properly. The position achieved in the rock back will determine how the athlete is presented to the bar and how the clearance (or failure) proceeds.

Summary

At the last stride before take-off the right hand on the pole is taken from hip level to the high position in preparation for take-off. The athlete should run fast and keep his hips and shoulders square to the front. The pole should be planted early, with the take-off (left) foot directly under the top (right) hand. The left arm should begin to brace (but not push the vaulter back and away from the pole at take-off) to act as the shock absorber, keeping the chest away from the pole. If the arm collapses here and allows the chest to hit the pole, any chances of a successful vault are effectively prevented.

Whilst the athlete is actively springing off the ground with the left leg, the free leg is driving vigorously forwards and upwards. The vaulter then enters the swinging phase, the initial bend on the pole having been achieved by the active take-off and correct posture. The vaulter should hang long, with a good distance between the top hand and the left foot.

The rock back then commences, where the aim is to get the left toes to the top of the pole. Another aim is to achieve a position where the vaulter can take most advantage of the unbending of the pole, when the stored energy in the pole is given back to the vaulter. Novice vaulters often try to leave the pole early here and shoot their legs towards the bar.

After rock back the vaulter continues his upward movement, endeavouring to pull along the long axis of the pole without trying to turn too early to face the bar with hips and chest. When the pull on the pole ceases the push begins, so that the athlete can achieve maximum distance between his top hand and his centre of gravity as it passes over the bar.

EQUIPMENT

One of the greatest problems of present day pole vaulting is that it can be a very exclusive activity because of the cost of vaulting poles. As a novice progresses, he can need as many as three or four poles a year. This is because the pole an athlete uses needs to be matched to his height, his body weight and his ability. Poles are made by various companies in lengths between ten and seventeen feet (3.05 and 5.18m). These various length poles are also weight rated, to the approximate weight of the athlete. Thus a beginner would choose a pole rated near his own body weight, whilst an expert, because of his runway speed and excellent vaulting ability, would use a pole rated well above his own body weight.

If a vaulter selects a pole which he cannot bend it is said to be too stiff and if he selects a pole below his body weight it is said to be too soft. If a pole which is equal to or greater than an athlete's body weight appears to be too soft, this probably means that the vaulter is becoming technically more efficient. Using a soft pole is not a good idea because it feels 'mushy' and after it is bent during a vault the pole unbends and returns its energy in a very slow and not very useful manner. Vaulters should also note that a fibreglass pole has a natural bend which is produced during manufacture. The vaulter must hold the pole so that the natural bend works in his favour. If it is held incorrectly the pole will not act as it should. When the pole is purchased, place each end on a hurdle and the natural bend will be apparent. Mark this bend on the pole with a fibre tipped pen. Then, place the pole in the planting box. Ensure that the bend points in the correct direction and then grip the pole. Bring the pole down and hold it as it will be carried on the approach run. The natural bend is now aligned properly.

Ideally a vaulter should use a pole which is just right for his physical and technical level. The expert vaulter will have a number of poles to take account of both adverse and favourable weather conditions. The novice vaulter who is considering buying a pole should take expert advice because poles, and thus mistakes, are very expensive. The best plan, when possible, is to join a regular vaulting group where a pool of poles is available for communal use. Poles rarely break nowadays. If they do, it is usually because athletes abuse them through lack of care.

Modern pole vaulting cannot take place without adequate landing areas. Before vaulting, remove the weather sheet and check that the area is completely safe. A good training aid is an elastic bar such as the one made by Kay-Metzeler. This can be placed on the uprights permanently for a training session and means that time is not wasted on bar replacement. However, athletes should occasionally use a hard bar in training. Once a training session is over replace the weather sheet on the landing area.

For competition, the athlete should equip himself with markers for the approach run, tape for the grip on the pole and some form of sticky substance, usually Venice turpentine, to improve his grip on the pole.

4 The High Jump

The high jump is another event that has undergone much technical development during recent decades. The improvement in landing areas is one of the principal factors. The earliest type of landing area was grass. In fact the athlete took off from grass and landed on it on the other side of the bar. As organisers began to take pity on the plight of high jumpers who were breaking the occasional limb, they improved the landing area by piling sand on the other side of the high jump uprights. Then as greater heights were cleared, the sand was piled higher still. Eventually, with the invention of the Fosbury flop, soft foam landing areas had to be used to prevent crippling injuries to high jumpers.

In the early days, when landing areas were either non-existent or just plain dangerous, techniques took account of self preservation on landing. In the scissors style the athlete cleared the bar in a trunk upright position and was very careful to look where he was landing. At the moment of clearance most of his body was above the bar, which was a mechanically inefficient position. The Eastern cut-off gave a more efficient layout over the bar and still allowed the athlete to see where he was landing. This style was then replaced by the Western roll, which gave a more efficient bar clearance position and allowed an angled approach to the bar, rather than the straight-on approach used by Eastern cut-off athletes. The straddle also employed an angled approach and a still more efficient bar clearance position.

The straddle, a sophisticated technique that needed a lot of strength in the take-off leg and excellent coaching knowledge to perfect, was used until recent times. In 1968 Dick Fosbury used his 'flop', with a curved approach run and a back layout bar clearance position, to win the Olympic title and revolutionise thinking on high jump. Now almost all high jumpers use the flop technique. Essentially it is a crude, easy to learn style, but a soft foam landing area must be used and the precise take-off point determined to prevent injury.

LEARNING TO HIGH JUMP

Fosbury flop has an efficient bar clearance position and is quite easy to learn, given the correct equipment. Use a good landing area, together with high jump stands and an elastic bar and a round section metal or fibreglass bar. In the early stages of learning the elastic bar is best. The metal and fibreglass bars hurt if the athlete hits or lands on them, whereas the rubber bar does not and gives more confidence to the novice jumper.

Scissors Jump

The first stage is to do a simple scissors jump, after deciding which foot the athlete takes off from. This can be determined by putting the bar at a very low height. The athlete then runs up to the bar from a head-on start and takes off to clear the bar

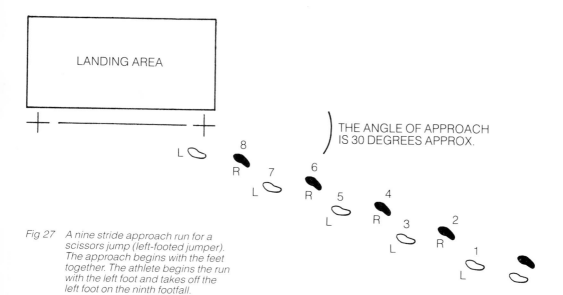

LANDING AREA

THE ANGLE OF APPROACH
IS 30 DEGREES APPROX.

*Fig 27   A nine stride approach run for a
scissors jump (left-footed jumper).
The approach begins with the feet
together. The athlete begins the run
with the left foot and takes off the
left foot on the ninth footfall.*

on whichever foot comes naturally. Several
jumps should be done to confirm which is
the best take-off foot. Teaching the
scissors, which has many good points that
can be transferred to the Fosbury flop, can
then begin.

Those who take off from their left foot will
take off from the right-hand side of the
landing area, as it is viewed from head on.
Right-footers jump from the other side. In
scissors, as in flop, the jumper takes off
from the foot furthest away from the bar.
Jumpers should be placed on a line which
is approximately thirty degrees to the bar
and they should use a gradually accelerating nine stride approach run. From the
outset athletes should talk to themselves
as they run along the approach, to
encourage a rythym. Divide the approach
into two parts and say – 'one, two, three,
four, one, two, three, four, lift'. The lift is
when the take-off foot hits the ground for
the take-off. The following points will help
to improve the scissors jump.

1. Start the approach run slowly and
accelerate. If the run is too fast, the athlete
will 'skate' through the take-off and get
very little lift into the air.
2. At take-off, ensure that the take-off foot
is in front of the hip and the hip is in front
of the shoulder. This encourages a desirable lean back at take-off.
3. At take-off there must be a firm plant of
the take-off foot.
4. At take-off swing the 'free' (i.e. non
take-off leg) strongly upwards, to help with
the lift.
5. At take-off keep the shoulder nearest
the bar high – do not let it lean in towards
the bar.

These points will also be very useful when
the flop is learned.

By learning the scissors many good
technical points will be understood and
confidence gained. It is no coincidence
that many top class flop high jumpers use
the scissors style in their warm-up before

Fig 28   A back flip onto a soft foam landing
area. Flex your knees and sit down
with a flat back.

Fig 29   Do not stretch the throat in the
arched position.

competitions. When the athlete is ready to progress, the first steps in learning the flop can commence.

Back Flip *(Figs 28 to 31)*

Begin by trying to back flip onto a soft foam landing area, as in *Figs 28 to 31*. Here the athlete is seen jumping over a bar, but to start with it can be done without. The following points will encourage successful jumping.

1. Flex the knees and sit down in preparation for take-off, with a flat back. If your head is forward and your bottom sticks out, you will not reach the landing

area and injury will result.

2. Keep a good arched position. Do not stretch the throat – keep the chin on the chest.

3. Lift the shoulders, head and feet up, to stop the feet dragging the bar off, and prepare for a landing on the top half of your back.

4. Aim to jump as far across the pit as possible, as well as jumping as high as possible, to achieve a safe landing in the middle of the area.

As the athlete becomes familiar with this activity, confidence will improve and the bars – preferably the elastic one – can be raised. Sometimes the athlete can jump

Fig 30   Lift the shoulders, head and feet to prevent the feet dragging the bar off.

Fig 31   Land safely on the top half of your back.

from a greater height, perhaps from a gym bench, but it must be firmly anchored to the ground to ensure safety. By jumping from a greater height, the athlete spends longer in the air and can learn to alter body shape more easily as he passes over the bar.

Approach Run and Take-off
(Figs 32 to 41)

Now the athlete must learn to take off, flop fashion, from a curved approach run. Essentially, a curved run is used to ensure:

1. That the inside shoulder travels vertically during take-off and during the first part of the athlete's flight in the air.

2. That rotation around the long axis of the body takes place during and after take-off.

It will be remembered that when learning the scissors jump a nine stride approach, divided into four strides, then five strides was used. In the flop the same division with the same rhythm is used. However, in the flop, the first four strides take place along a straight line and the last five into take-off take place along a curved line.

The curved approach can be practised by drawing a circle of seven metre (7.7 yard) radius on the high jump fan. The left-footed take-off jumper then runs anti-clockwise round the circle (the right-footed jumper runs clockwise) and takes off every five strides. During this exercise the

Fig 32 The curved part of the approach has begun.

Fig 33 An appreciable lean-in is seen.

Fig 34 Running speed is maintained . . .

Fig 35 . . . with arm action still emphasised.

Fig 36   In this final take-off stride . . .

Fig 37   . . . the right foot is in front of the hip and the hip is in front of the shoulder.

Fig 38   Excellent vertical lift is the result . . . .

Fig 39   . . . with a good bar clearance position.

jumper should again talk to himself, saying 'one, two, three, four, lift' on each footfall into take-off. As well as this activity the jumper can also run around the circle leaning inwards towards the centre, to simulate the correct posture required during those last five strides into take-off. When the athlete is doing the five stride approach into take-off, the following points should be emphasised.

1. Lean in to the centre of the circle.
2. At the moment of take-off (as in scissors style) ensure that the take-off foot is in front of the hip and the hip is in front of the shoulder, giving a lean back position.
3. Swing the free leg up, bent at the knee,

Fig 40 The arms and head are lifted as she leaves the bar, ensuring that the heels and calves do not drag the bar off.

Fig 41 She lands on her back in a comfortable position.

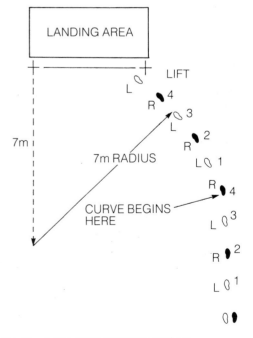

Fig 42 A nine stride approach run for a 'flop' high jumper (left-footed take-off).

to give better vertical lift. Ensure that the knee of the free leg is opposite the hip at the moment of take-off.

Once these points have been learned, the proper approach for the flop can be set out and the full technique practised. *Fig 42* shows a plan of a typical approach run of nine strides. There are four strides along a straight line and five strides on the curve. The seven metres radius curve for the last activity is also explained. In practice, top class jumpers use a wider radius than seven metres, but for beginners and improvers seven metres is adequate.

Before the athlete actually does his first proper flop jump the rhythm of the approach run should be practised. These adjustments are summarised as follows:

1. The run begins with the athlete leaning forwards.
2. By the time the athlete has completed four strides he should be in an upright posture.
3. At the beginning of the curve (the fifth stride in the approach run) he should be leaning in towards the centre of the curve.
4. At the time of take-off, the athlete will be leaning in towards the centre of the circle and leaning backwards in preparation for take-off.
5. At the moment of take-off, ensure that the take-off foot is kept in line with the shin. If the foot is turned away from the bar (everted), then ankle injury can result.

Fig 43 The last three strides of the approach, showing postural changes.

Fig 44 Note the lean in.

Fig 45 Notice the hips sink, in preparation for the spring into take-off.

Summary

Aim for a good take-off position with the left foot in front of its hip and the hip in front of its shoulder, resulting in an excellent lean back. If you lean away from the bar at take-off you should achieve a good vertical lift. After take-off the knee of the free leg should work vigorously upwards and continue to do so until the bar clearance begins. The shoulder nearest the bar

Fig 46 At the moment of take-off, ensure that the take-off foot is kept in line with the shin.

Fig 47 Aggressive running in an upright position.

Fig 48 *In preparation for take-off . . .*

Fig 49 *. . . the athlete begins the lean back . . .*

Fig 50 *. . . ready for the lift into the air.*

Fig 51 *The hips sink . . .*

Fig 52   . . . and the arms realign, ready for
          the double arm action.

Fig 53   The athlete gathers . . .

Fig 54   . . . and tension is seen in the take-off leg.

Fig 55   The right leg drives vigorously upwards . . .

Fig 56 ... to aid vertical lift.

Fig 57 A good bar clearance position is achieved ...

Fig 58 ... with the arms and head moving upwards ...

Fig 59 ... to bring the lower part of the legs clear of the bar.

Fig 60   A safe landing follows . . .

Fig 61   . . . with the forces being absorbed
on the back.

is also kept high during this phase. The head should not be thrown backwards during clearance. This means that the lower legs will not drop too low during the bar clearance phase, so allowing the legs to be brought quickly away from the bar. To aid clearance of the bar lift the head, shoulders and arms upwards. Dragging the bar off with the calves or the heels is always a problem in high jumping and a vigorous action in this phase always helps. The final landing is made on the back, presenting as large an area of the body as possible to give a comfortable landing.

EQUIPMENT

Because of the particular demands of the high jump take-off the high jumper needs a special shoe. Rules for high jump shoes are different from the rules for track shoes. High jumpers are allowed a maximum of six spikes in the sole and four in the heel of their shoe, to give a good, firm footing during take-off. The high jumper is also allowed longer spikes than the track athlete, twelve millimetres rather than nine millimetres.

In the track bag, high jumpers should carry tape to mark their approach run and a marker which will stick firmly into the surface without damaging it, to show the beginning of their run.

5   The Long Jump

Long jumping is the simplest of the four jumps to perform. In order to participate, athletes do not need to use expensive equipment or sophisticated techniques. The very simple equation of speed on the approach run, accuracy on and lift from the take-off board and an efficient landing has won many prizes for athletes. Athletes often spend hours perfecting a particular technique, but the most important considerations are running speed, accuracy on the take-off board and 'bouncy' legs to give lift from the take-off board. Good jumping technique will never take the place of these desirable physical qualities. In recent years the ladies' world record has been improved upon by athletes whose technique in the air is not particularly good. However their running action into take-off, the take-off itself and landing techniques have been brilliant.

LEARNING TO LONG JUMP

Having said that the long jump is an uncomplicated event, teaching should start from simplicity. Newcomers to the event need not be introduced to the take-off board until the later stages of teaching. To begin with, athletes should be taught to think of speed and lift at take-off.

Choose a suitable jumping area, a long jump pit itself which should be jumped into sideways if it is wide enough. If it is not wide enough, use it in the conventional manner. Mark out a short approach run and place a marker where the run starts. Athletes should not go further back than this mark. At this stage, if athletes do a lot of jumps from a long run fatigue will set in very quickly and destroy any semblance of quality jumping. From this short approach (seven strides is sufficient) run, take off then land in whatever style comes naturally.

As athletes jump, the following fundamental points should be introduced:

1. Run fast.
2. In the take-off aim for a natural head position, a flat back, extension of the take-off leg, correct position of the free leg and vigorous use of the arms (*Fig 62* is an excellent illustration of these points.) Once these postural positions are achieved, look at the action of the take-off leg. This should be a 'fast foot' action which is first pawing and then driving as the athlete extends the take-off leg.
3. At this point the action in the air should be natural and most athletes will do the 'sail' style.
4. On landing, the aim is to reach out with the heels as far as possible to produce a good 'leg shoot'.

These are the fundamental points of long jumping which will enable athletes to jump a long way.

Approach Run

Before considering technique in the air, the approach run must be examined in detail. In the early stages of learning the long jump a short approach is used, so that athletes do not tire quickly and can concentrate on the jump itself. In a full approach long jump, athletes must accelerate and reach top speed as they take off. The length of the approach varies according to age, physical maturity and physical ability and is outlined in the chapter on pole vaulting.

As well as speed on the runway, rhythm is another important aspect. In the early part of the approach, speed is gradually generated. Then, over the last five strides (seven for more mature athletes) the legs actually speed up in a quicker rhythm into an attack on the board. To see this point well illustrated, the reader should observe a top class jumper in action.

In the approach run, jumpers need to be in the correct posture at take-off. Jumpers begin their run by leaning forwards and by the end of the run they are in an upright position. The upright position should be achieved as early as possible in the approach run. *Fig 7* shows the total relationship between postural adjustment, speed and rhythm on the runway.

Accuracy of approach is also very necessary because the jump is measured from the scratch line. If the jump is made from over that line it is a no jump and if it is made from behind the jumper loses distance. Jumpers must realise that it is a great skill to run from as far as thirty or forty metres away and then place the take-off foot as close to the scratch line as is possible. Much practice is required.

So, on the approach run the important words are speed, rhythm, posture and

Fig 62   The take-off position in the long jump.

accuracy. Accuracy is achieved in the following way:

1. Establish which is the take-off foot.
2. With the back to the jumping pit, place the non take-off foot up to the scratch line and begin running the required number of strides (fifteen, for example) back along the runway.
3. Where the fifteenth stride falls, place a marker.
4. When rested, place the non take-off foot by this marker and run back towards the take-off board and take off. Have an observer mark the fifteenth footfall in relation to the take-off board.
5. If the take-off foot was over the board, move the start marker back the corresponding amount. If the foot was behind the board, move the marker forwards.

Final accuracy can only be achieved by repeating points 4 and 5 above. Remember that weather and track conditions can change and so alter the length of approach. If an athlete runs fifteen strides with the wind, then against the wind, the actual measurement of each fifteen strides will change considerably. Thus, the athlete must be prepared for change every time he jumps.

6. Once consistency of run-up has been achieved in training, it must be measured so that it is transferable to any runway. Put the heel to the scratch line and measure the run-up as a number of foot lengths. Make sure that the heel and toe always go together for absolute accuracy. Note the measurement in the training diary.

7. Top class jumpers usually use only one mark for accuracy. Another mark is usually placed some five to seven strides from the take-off board as a 'cue' to denote where the legs have to speed up and the attack on the board begins. Athletes build up towards top speed at the cue mark. Thereafter, they try to achieve 'fast legs' into and through take-off. This builds speed and rhythm into the approach run.

A lot of time should be spent on the approach run in training, because it will reap rich rewards in competition. Athletes who are not the quickest sprinters can make up for speed deficiencies by practising the technical points of the run-up.

Technique in the Air

In long jumping much has been written about technique in the air. Should the athlete use sail, hang, 1½ hitch kick or 2½ hitch kick? Some thought that the answer to jumping long distances was to use an 'advanced' technique, but this is not so. To jump long distances we return to the equation mentioned earlier of: *speed + lift at take-off + an efficient landing = distance*. The utilisation of good technique in the air particularly affects one factor – the efficient landing.

When the athlete takes off there is a checking, which causes a forward rotation about the centre of gravity. If allowed to develop, it results in an awful landing position. This rotation cannot be completely prevented, but it can be slowed down to give a more efficient landing position. The slowing down of this rotation is achieved by adopting a long position in the air as in *Figs 67 (13)* and *70 (4)*. This has led to the development of the styles of long jumping mentioned earlier.

Long Jump Styles

The Sail

This is the simplest form of jump. Usually the athlete goes through the good take-off position and then tucks the knees up into the chest. This actually speeds up the rotation about the centre of gravity and produces the worst possible landing position. This style should not be used because of the inefficient landing position it produces.

The Hang (Figs 63 to 68)

After going through the good take-off position the athlete drops the free leg to the vertical and it is joined by the take-off leg. The arms go overhead to achieve the long position, which leads to the slowing down of rotation about the centre of gravity. The jumper travels a long way in this position, then prepares for landing by

Fig 64   The preparation for take-off, where the hips sink lower than in the
          normal sprinting stride.

Fig 66   A very good drive of the take-off leg and the free leg. Note the
          stable, flat back and good head position in number 12.

Fig 68   The legs continue through and the heels are pushed forwards for a good 'leg
          shoot'. A good landing position results.

Fig 63   The 'hang' style of long jumping: Beverley Kinch showing a fine sprinting action on the runway.

Fig 65   Take-off preparation continues. Kinch's arm action is weak in this phase; the right arm should be driving back, flexed at the elbow.

Fig 67   A good long position in number 13, and then the 'hang shape' is adopted. The legs are brought through well in preparation for landing.

The Long Jump

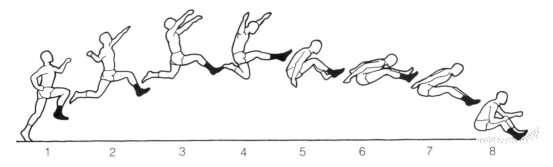

Fig 69   The 'stride' style of long jumping.

lifting the legs upwards and forwards and lowers the trunk. The arms should swing past the legs during landing to ensure a good leg shoot. *Figs 63 to 68*, showing Beverly Kinch, the British record holder at 6.90 metres, illustrate the hang.

The Stride Jump (Fig 69)

This term has come into use in recent years through styles used in East Germany. In this style, the athlete maintains the take-off position for as long as possible. As the athlete comes in to land, the take-off leg joins the free leg for a better landing position.

The Hitch Kick (Fig 70)

In the hitch kick the athlete still achieves the basic take-off position and then continues to stride in the air, achieving the long position necessary to ensure a good landing. Athletes can do a 1½ stride hitch kick or a 2½ stride hitch kick. The 2½ demands that the athlete has very good lift off the board after take-off, so that he has time to complete the necessary actions in the air. In the hitch kick, forward leg movements are done flexed at the knee and backward movements with the legs straight. The arms move in sequence with the opposite leg and then come together for the final landing.

Fig 70   The 1½ hitch kick .

Summary

By the final two strides a very high speed should be achieved. The penultimate stride is slightly longer than the preceding ones, with the hips lowering slightly in preparation for the spring off the board. At this stage of the approach the athlete must always think of high hips, even though they do actually sink. The final stride is a shorter stride, where effort is put into take-off. The leg action onto and away from the board should be thought of as a fast pawing action of the foot. During the final stride the elbow opposite the take-off leg should be driven backwards. The take-off position should have good head and leg positions, and a strong, flat back. During flight, allow the free leg to drop down long, after achieving the 'knee opposite hip' position. The left leg moves forward bent at the knee, and the right leg then joins it to prepare for landing. Athletes should avoid getting into the hang position too early, pushing their stomachs forwards immediately after take-off, without going into a strong 'knee opposite hip' position first.

6 The Triple Jump

Along with the pole vault, the triple jump is the most technical of the jumps. It is unique in that it must be done in a particular manner, which is laid down in rule 86 (i) in the AAA rule book. This rule must be understood before the event is learned, because it determines the exact manner by which the event should proceed. If this procedure is incorrect, the judges will declare a no jump. The rule says: *'The hop shall be made so that the competitor shall first land on the same foot with which he shall have taken off. In the step he shall land on the other foot, from which subsequently the jump is performed'*. There is also a second part to this rule which says: *'If a competitor while jumping touches the ground with the 'sleeping' leg, it shall be considered a failure'*.

The triple jump used to be called the hop, step and jump and the 'sleeping' leg means the free swinging leg in each phase. This explains the terminology of the rule. It is very difficult to understand why this part of the rule was made. If the 'sleeping' leg does strike the ground, it actually hinders the jumper and certainly will not assist him.

LEARNING TO TRIPLE JUMP

The first task is to understand the rule of procedure for the triple jump. Athletes will find that they have a preferred and stronger leg and this will be used in the first phase take-off and landing. Usually,

this is the leg which is used for long jumping. The second phase landing is made with the 'weaker' leg (although through training the 'weak' leg should be made as strong as the preferred leg). The final phase is done in the usual long jump manner.

Begin learning in a very steady way, putting the left foot on the ground and doing a standing triple jump. Take off the left and land on the left, then land on the right, then land with the feet together. Keep the movement continuous. Build the rhythm *left–left–right–together*. If this feels strange, start with the right foot in a *right–right–left–together* rhythm. It is important to learn the correct foot placement and jumping rhythm first, before progressing to a triple jump run-up with an approach run. The triple jump can be very demanding on the legs and landing forces are quite high. Begin steadily and learn the fundamentals first. Once the correct procedure laid down by the rules has been learned, further fundamental ideas must be understood.

The second task is to learn the concept of the three equal phases of the triple jump. In fact, for the beginner the whole effort is usually divided into thirty-seven per cent for the first phase, twenty-six per cent for the second phase and thirty-seven per cent for the final phase. However, when learning, think of three equal phases so that the correct concept is understood. If this is not done, you will produce a typical novice jump of a very large hop, a tiny step and a very large jump, giving

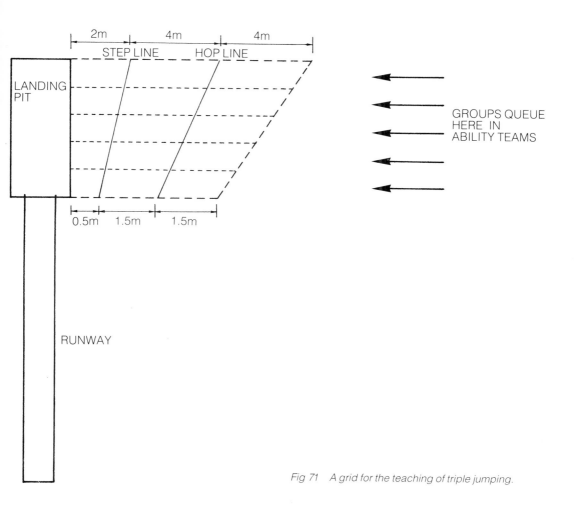

Fig 71   A grid for the teaching of triple jumping.

a diminished total distance. Think of three equal phases to start with to give the longest jumps. Once this concept is understood, a grid can be marked out, adjacent to the triple jump pit as shown in *Fig 71*. This can be used for standing jumps or jumps from a short approach run. Which lines are used will depend upon the ability of the athlete. It is sensible to begin on the narrower markings and progress

steadily. The grid might have one drawback. Because lines are marked on the grass, athletes will tend to look down to the markings, thus affecting good jumping posture. Ensure that the back is flat and the head is held up.

The third task is to learn to land on the foot correctly. When a triple jumper lands, it is slightly heel-first, but the athlete will feel that it is a flat foot landing. Toe-first landings are dangerous and unstable and injury will probably result.

The fourth task to learn, which is really the secret of successful triple jumping, is the manner in which the foot is presented to the ground during take-offs and landings. Jarring landings, painful backs, ankles and feet all result from poor action of the foot and lower leg. The action is a 'reaching and pawing' one, where as the athlete comes in to land his foot moves forwards and then sharply backwards as the foot hits the ground. The reaching and pawing action is easily learned through 'stepping' – jumping from left foot to right foot to left foot and so on, over ten ground contacts. This process can be furthered by doing the activities in the jumps decathlon (*see Fig 113*). These tables are used for various forms of competition, but the activities are excellent for learning the technical points of triple jump.

When this stage has been reached, the athlete will understand the basic principles of triple jumping and must now move to the runway to do proper triple jumping, ready for competition. It has already been explained that landing forces increase drastically when athletes jump off a fast approach run. Athletes who collapse on landing after a fast approach should restrict themselves to short approaches and build up their strength. The process of determining the length, rhythm, speed and postural adjustments on the runway is exactly the same as that described for the pole vault in Chapter 3.

There is one fundamental difference between the long jump and the triple jump and that occurs at the end of the approach run. In the long jump the athlete needs as much height as possible off the board, combined with a high running speed, to gain maximum distance. In the triple jump,

after the first take-off, he lands and takes off again twice more. These landings slow the forward progress of the triple jumper. Therefore, in order to maintain as high a speed as possible during the three phases, the triple jumper takes off with a shallower angle in comparison with the long jumper. The triple jumper strives to drive out and away from the board, whereas the long jumper strives for height.

Competition techniques of triple jumpers vary. In the past, techniques have been attributed to certain nations – the Polish technique versus the Russian technique – or to certain body types – the flat technique for the faster athlete versus the steep technique for the slower, stronger athlete. It is always best to fit the technique to the athlete, to take account of the athlete's strengths and weaknesses. It is wrong to fit the athlete to the technique, because a particular athlete may not have the physical and technical qualities demanded by that technique. Having noted that there are variants, the following points are important to basic technique.

Arm Action

All good jumpers maintain an alternate arm action, as seen in the normal running stride, up to the take-off board. There are a number of arm action variations displayed by triple jumpers after they complete the first take-off; these are:

1. Alternate action through the jump.
2. Alternate action into the first landing, then double arm action into and through the second landing.
3. Alternate action off the board, re-aligning into double arm action through the following phases.

4. Double arm action throughout, aligning the arm into double shift before the board. This fourth method should not be copied, even though some top class athletes use it, because it slows the athlete in his approach run.

The Three Phases
(Figs 72 to 79)

The approach into the first phase will have been as fast as possible, with an emphasis on an increase in leg speed and the maintenance of high hips during the last three strides. Arm action will have remained in alternate phase before take-off.

At the first take-off the foot lands slightly heel-first, but the athlete will feel that it is a flat-footed contact. The take-off is executed dynamically, with the free thigh and the opposite arm driving forwards. The knee of the free leg should reach hip level before its sweep backwards and downwards as a long limb. After take-off is completed, the take-off leg is picked up in true hopping fashion, with the knee opposite the hip and the thigh parallel to the ground. From this position the leg is ready for active landing at the end of the first phase in the 'reaching and pawing' action. As this happens, the free leg swings through vigorously into the second phase.

The second phase (the step) is characterised by the wide thigh split, with the legs bent at the knees during flight. The aim is to hold the active leg with the thigh parallel to the ground, in preparation for the 'reaching and pawing' action at the end of the second phase. During each landing and take-off, the action is complemented by the swinging of the arms and the vigorous swing through of the free leg. Landing strains on the legs are very high,

as is speed loss if the landing is poor.

In the third phase the athlete salvages what is left of horizontal speed. The free leg is again swung through vigorously from the second phase into the final jump take-off. The jumper must give particular emphasis to vertical lift at this point. The time in the air is so short in this phase, especially with novice jumpers, that there is little point in attempting a sophisticated long jump type technique. The emphasis is solely upon foot speed through the landing and take-off and the correct body posture to give vertical lift in the correct direction. The execution of a simple sail or hang style is usually sufficient to give a good final landing.

The aim at final landing is to get the feet as far ahead of the body as possible, without falling back into the sand and losing distance. An increasing number of modern jumpers use a 'skid through' technique on landing at the end of the third phase. By using this method, the athlete tries to reach as far forward as possible with the feet, yet not mark the sand with the buttocks. When done well, the athlete collapses his knees on landing and arches the back to prevent the buttocks hitting the sand. When done badly, the 'skid through' method can lose athletes a lot of distance. Agile athletes seem to be able to use this method successfully.

Summary

The arms should move from single phase into take-off, moving to the double arm shift. The arms should synchronise with the legs throughout. The leg technique should be a 'reaching and pawing' action. In mid phase the active thigh should be held parallel to the ground, with a wide split between the thighs. This allows a vigorous swing through of the rear leg into the next phase. During all three phases, the trunk should be held upright so

Fig 72   The athlete sprints at top speed into take off, with a vigorous drive . . .

Fig 74   Note the thigh parallel position (left). The foot reaches for the landing . . .

Fig 73 . . . into the first phase, the hop. The free leg drops into a long
position, as the hopping leg prepares for the landing.

Fig 75 . . . and is pulled back sharply in a 'pawing' action. The body accepts its weight
and reacts, driving the athlete into the next phase, the step.

Fig 76   In mid-step there is a wide split of the thighs and the left thigh is held parallel to the ground. The 'reaching and pawing' action is also seen in the landing.

Fig 78   A 'sail' style is used with a good leg shoot . . .

Fig 77   A good take-off position into the final jump.

Fig 79   . . . into a poor skid through landing.

The Triple Jump

that balance is maintained. During the take-off the trunk should be in a good, stable position and the free leg and the arms should work vigorously upwards. The landings should be made on a flat foot, which lands very slightly heel-first.

7   Training

Track and field athletics in Britain is a very successful sport both at international level and at the grass roots. One of the reasons for that success is the seriousness with which athletes treat the planning of training in relation to competition demands. 'If something is worth doing, it is worth doing well' the old adage tells us. This could be adopted as the saying which is most relevant to all our athletes. Training, although enjoyable, must be done properly if performance is to improve.

Anyone, regardless of standard, can improve their performance if training and preparation for competition is done systematically and thoughtfully. It is not possible to computerise training programmes and produce a standard 'formula' for one event, because each athlete is unique. The training method used by one individual will not have the same effects and results on another. Each athlete must have his unique training programme which takes account of his particular strengths and weaknesses. In that training programme there will be many common factors which all high jumpers, triple jumpers, long jumpers or pole vaulters might use, but a training schedule must cater for the needs of the individual athlete.

PLANNING TRAINING

An understanding of how to plan training is important. This planning should be done by the coach with beginner and novice athletes. As the athlete gets older and wiser, the planning can be done in discussion with the coach so that ideas are pooled.

The athlete's training year is divided into three parts, preparation, competition and transition. The transition period is the rest between the end of one competition period and the beginning of the next preparation period. The popular name now given to the planning of training is *periodisation*, which is a systematic and progressive approach to an athlete's preparation for a competition peak.

In general terms, periodisation of training can be compared to the building of a house. Training is like building a foundation on which the walls and finally the roof can be fixed. Without strong foundations the walls and roof will eventually collapse. In athletics terms the foundations of fitness are built in the winter preparation periods. The benefits of that work are seen in the competitive periods in the summer.

It is very important for athletes to do the correct work at a particular time in the year. Heavy plodding repetitions are best done in early preparation, whilst quick, light, fast work is ideal for producing good competition performances. In preparation periods the volume of work will be high and the intensity of training low. Then follows a systematic transition to the competition period where the volume of work is low and the intensity high. For those readers wishing to learn more about periodisation of training, specialist publications on this topic are mentioned at the back of this book.

Young developing athletes are very special people. They should never be treated as scaled-down adults. A young triple jumper who is half the age of Willie Banks, the world record holder, should not do half Banks' training schedule! He should have a specially designed schedule, which takes into account his strengths, weaknesses and stage of development. Young athletes have their own features of growth and development and need special treatment. In the jumping events the development of technique and speed will be paramount.

Training Sessions

Each individual training session must follow a simple, logical pattern, which is detailed below.

1. Warm up. Jog two to four laps of the grass infield of the track, to generate body warmth.
2. General mobility exercises. Choose one exercise for each part of the body, up to six. The BAAB book *Mobility Training* shows a vast number of exercises.
3. Special mobility exercises. Choose exercises specific to your event. Specific exercises for jumpers, for the legs and hips, are shown in *Figs 80 to 89* .
4. Technical activities.
5. Fitness work.
6. Warm down. Jog two to four laps of the infield on grass to settle down mentally and physically after the training session.

Note that technical training should always come before fitness work in the training session, because it is difficult to produce technical excellence when the body is fatigued.

Fig 80   Hamstring stretch .

Fig 81   Hurdling type exercise for the hip.

Fig 82   Hurdle seated position to mobilise the hip joint, lower back and hamstring. Repeat
exercise with the left leg forward and the right to the side.

Fig 83   Loose swinging of the leg from right to left and back for hip mobility. Change legs to
exercise the other side of the body.

Fig 84   Hip mobility exercise for the adductors and abductors.

Fig 85   Hip mobility exercise.

Fig 86   Hip mobility and hamstring exercise.

Fig 87 Hip mobility exercise.

Fig 88 Hamstring and lower back exercise – this must be done slowly.

Fig 89 Hip, hamstring and quadriceps stretch; change legs to exercise both sides of the body.

TRAINING ACTIVITIES

Training schedules should demand that athletes move from general training to specific training, from preparation periods through to competition periods. With that general principle in mind, here are some specific training activities which jumpers could use. Athletes should always seek good advice from a qualified BAAB coach in their search for the ideal schedule.

Two major points should be noted first. Training activities which involve athletes going into and remaining in deep oxygen debt during a training session should be left out entirely. Secondly, strength training can be undertaken but it should be undertaken carefully. Young athletes' spines should not be overloaded with heavy weight training bars. Physically immature bodies should not be subjected to such treatment. Strength work should be in the form of *light* hopping and bounding, which develops specific jumping strength, and circuit training which develops cardio-vascular and local muscular endurance.

The following summary will help in the planning of a training programme.

1. Identify the competition period.
2. Identify the important competitions within that period.
3. Divide the year into preparation, competition and transition.
4. Identify the particular aspects of fitness required in a particular training period (for example speed, strength, endurance and so on).
5. Identify the methods required to produce that fitness.
6. Estimate the time available for training.
7. Plan the scheme of work.

With those principles in mind, the following training activities are recommended.

Running Endurance

The aim is to develop cardio-vascular efficiency. It also helps with preliminary conditioning of the legs.

Distance Running (Preparation Periods)

Long distance to some athletes is one mile and to others thirty miles! The novice athlete should run for five minutes without stopping and then turn around and return to his starting point. This can be developed progressively over the preparation period into a fifty or sixty minute run for the mature athlete. Heart rate should be approximately 150 beats per minute during the run, and the athlete should aim to run comfortably and without distress. Use firm grass surfaces wherever possible, to prevent foot injuries and ankle soreness.

Interval Running (Preparation Periods)

Follow the typical Gerschler/Reindell method. Mature athletes could start with a session of 10 × 200 metres in 32 seconds, with a 90 second jog recovery between each run, developing to two sets of 10 × 200 metres as fitness improves. Adaptation can be advanced as athletes progress, by decreasing the time of jog recovery between runs; increasing the speed of each run, or increasing the number of repetitions. (*See* BAAB book *Middle and Long Distance Marathon and Steeplechase* by Watts and Wilson.)

Interval training can be very boring. Sugar the pill by using environments away from the track. Devise continuous relays which produce the same physiological

Training

results as interval training. Remember that monotony deadens the spirit of an athlete.

Fartlek Training

This is a Swedish word meaning speed play. The athlete runs for a certain duration at varying intensities. There are long sustained sections, fast bursts, hill runs and even walking sections. The pace can vary according to the fitness of the athlete and how he feels. The running should be done in the countryside in an invigorating environment. As the jumper improves he must learn to increase the pressure on himself.

Strength Endurance

This is usually defined as 'the capacity to maintain the quality of the muscles' contractile force', and consists mainly of running activities. An athlete needs to be physically mature to undertake this type of training. Strength endurance can best be developed by using the following methods.

1. Hill running. Ideally this should be done over 150 to 200 metres up a fifteen degree incline. Local circumstances often dictate the distances and the inclines. Four repetitions in sets of one to four should be done according to the fitness of the athlete. There should be a jog back recovery between repetitions and two to five minutes between sets.
2. Sand hill running. Courses, repetitions and sets must be determined by the coach, according to the athlete and the local terrain.
3. Back-to-backs or turnabouts. A typical session might be two sets of four repetitions over 80 metres, with a thirty second turnaround and two to five minutes

between sets, according to the athlete. Each run should be undertaken at a high speed.
4. Harness running. The harness must be held by a responsible person, applying an appropriate resistance over distances up to thirty metres. The load will vary according to the athlete.
5. Tyre towing. Distances up to 100 metres can be used in repetitions and sets appropriate to the athlete. Higher loadings can be achieved by placing shot into the tyre casting.

Speed Endurance

This is defined as 'the capacity for co-ordinating the speed of contraction of the muscles, in the climate of endurance'. It is not often that a jumper calls upon this particular capacity in competition, but it is essential to acquire it as an aspect of the jumper's sprinting development. Long jumpers, triple jumpers and pole vaulters could use the following activities:

1. Flat out runs over 80 to 150 metres. There should be a complete rest recovery, with four to six repetitions.
2. 'Ins and outs' – runs over 80 to 150 metres. A rhythm of accelerate–decelerate–accelerate should be developed. The rhythm should be developed on the basis of the first forty per cent being acceleration, the next twenty per cent deceleration and the final forty per cent acceleration again. Six to eight repetitions in one or two sets is sufficient.

Pure Speed

The need for basic speed and runway specific speed has been mentioned many times already. Speed *can* be improved upon with the necessary work. Athletes who are not blessed with natural speed should not despair! Ideally, male athletes in the long jump, triple jump and pole vault should be capable of running faster than 10.50 seconds for 100 metres and 6.80 seconds for 60 metres indoors. Female athletes should be able to run faster than 11.80 seconds for 100 metres. The specifics of those sprint races, particularly the start and the first 20 metres, may prevent such times being recorded. However, that speed potential should be there. The following activities will help develop speed.

Acceleration Runs

These are done over 60 or 90 metres. The distance is split into thirds. A rhythm of accelerate, sprint fast, decelerate is practised over each third. The 60 metres distance is closely related to the actual approach run rhythm in the long jump, triple jump and pole vault, with a 20 metre build-up and a 20 metre attack to the board. Pole vaulters can do these repetitions with and without the pole.

Runway Sprinting

1. Rhythm runs, practising the aspects of accelerate and attack on the runway, over the full approach run distance. This is done without a take-off at the board, the sole aim being the development of rhythm in the early part of the approach and a high leg speed over the last five to seven strides from where the cue mark is placed. High jumpers must also practise rhythm runs, so that they reach their optimum speed during take-off.
2. Accuracy runs. These must always be practised with a full take-off. Accuracy

cannot be tested on a run-through without a take-off. It is only when a full take-off is executed, that the exact rhythm and postural adjustments take place.

For both accuracy and rhythm runs, six to eight repetitions should be enough, although there should be a full rest recovery between repetitions.

Strength

One definition of strength is 'the ability to exert force against a resistance'. The type of force and the type of resistance change from event to event in jumping. The training rule of specificity tells us to channel our training activities to the particular requirements of an event.

There are different types of strength which fall into the three broad divisions of maximum, elastic and endurance strength. In jumping and vaulting, elastic strength is high on the priority list. An athlete who develops this quality of strength will have the ability to take off and rebound into the next phase of the jump or vault. More importantly, he will have the ability to rebound very quickly and positively from those landings. Endurance strength will also be high on the priority list in preparation periods. This type of strength gives a good foundation on which other physical qualities can be built.

Maximum Strength

Maximum strength is a quality required by the jumper. To put it into context, gross strength has a high priority for a shot putter or discus thrower, but is low on the list for an endurance runner. A jumper's requirement falls into the middle area of this spectrum. Some time will be spent on developing maximum strength by the experienced jumper. However, it should be remembered that elastic strength is the most important strength determinant of performance in jumping.

Endurance Strength

This is the capacity of the body to withstand fatigue and the jumper must develop it in preparation periods and maintain it in the competition periods. Circuit training is a very important way of developing endurance strength. Circuits for general endurance can be devised as can specific circuits for the legs.

A suggested regime is as follows:

1. Choose six exercises relevant to the development of a jumper. Relevant exercises are illustrated in *Figs 90 to 95*; these are the hamstring curl, quadriceps curl, back raise (no higher than shown), star jump, inclined sit-ups and leg changes.
2. Do one exercise for thirty seconds, followed by a thirty second rest.
3. After each circuit, have a five minute rest. Do three circuits initially.

To increase the overload, as athletes get fitter, the following alternatives are available: do the exercises for a longer period; reduce the interval of rest; or increase the number of circuits according to the needs of the individual.

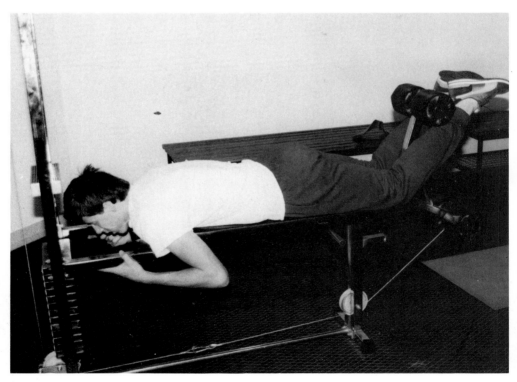

Fig 90   Hamstring curl – pull the heels to the buttocks and then lower them.

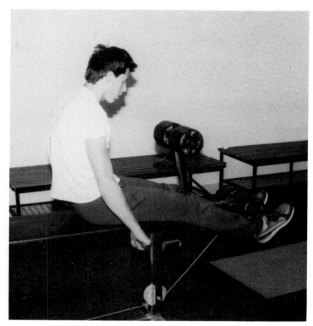

Fig 91   Quadriceps curl – extend the legs
         fully and then lower them.

Fig 92   Back raise – lift the head no higher
(*below*) than this position, then lower to the
         ground.

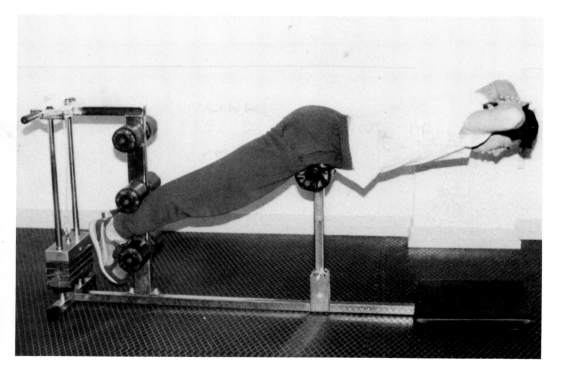

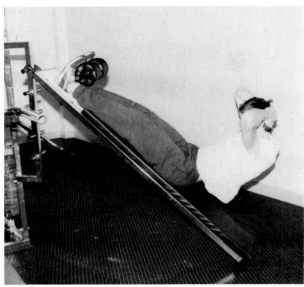

Fig 93
(above left)
Star jump – jump explosively to this position.

Fig 94
(above right)
Sit-up – this exercise can be done with various degrees of incline. To make it easier, make the bench angle less.

Fig 95
Leg changes – change legs vigorously back and forwards.

Elastic Strength

This type of strength is so called because activities which improve it affect the elastic and the contractile components of muscle. These components are developed by reflex contraction in the expression of strength at speed. There are two basic methods of developing this type of strength: hopping, bounding and multiple jumping activities, and weight training with bar and disc.

1. Hopping, Bounding and Multiple Jumps

Learning the technique of bounding is very important. The following points should be stressed in the initial stages:

1. The foot contact with the ground is not a pounding action, but the usual reaching and pawing action on flat foot.
2. The trunk and head must be upright during the jumps.
3. The hips must be properly aligned under the trunk – do not let the bottom stick out!
4. Arms should swing either alternately or in double fashion where appropriate for long jump, high jump or triple jump.

Develop bounding by using individual jumps such as: two hops, two steps and a jump; five spring jumps (bunny jumps); running five hops and a jump; and timed twenty-five metres hop.

After technique has been learned, activities can be put together as full sessions. The following are suggested sessions for preparation and competition periods.

Preparation Periods

Try the following activities.

1. Hopping on the left leg.
2. Hopping on the right leg.
3. Stepping.
4. Hop–hop–step–step rhythm.

Do twelve ground contacts of each activity, with a walk back recovery. This constitutes one set. Start with two sets and develop this to four or five in line with the physical maturity of the athlete.

Competition Periods

Use activities similar to those used in the preparation period, but confine the athlete to six ground contacts for each one rather than twelve. Undertake the bounding at this time of the year with a lighter and quicker touch.

Sophistications of bounding can include depth jumping – jumping down from a height never greater than seventy centimetres – and jumping wearing a weighted vest. This extra weight should never increase natural body weight by more than five per cent. *Fig 96* shows the use of gymnasium box-tops to jump down from and up to. The coach with initiative can develop local facilities, such as stadium steps, for his bounding activities. Similar sessions can also be used in the gymnasium, using exercises on the apparatus shown in *Fig 96*.

2. Weight Training with Bar and Disc

In weight training with the bar and disc, the experienced and physically mature jumper should aim to develop both maximum strength and elastic strength.

Fig 96   Examples of activities for jumpers with gymnasium equipment.

Fig 97 Step-up onto a bench – begin from a balanced position.

However, athletes should again heed the warning that strength is just one of the physical qualities required and is not the ultimate requirement. It must be developed in tandem with all other aspects of the schedule, especially speed and technique.

Qualities of strength can be developed by:

1. Lifting at 80 to 100 per cent of maximum, with one to five repetitions in three to five sets. For example, five lifts at 80 per cent, three at 95 per cent, one at 100 per cent, three at 95 per cent and five at 80 per cent. This represents one set. Three to five sets should be done according to the athlete.
2. Lifting at 70 to 85 per cent of maximum, with five to ten repetitions in three to five sets. For example, ten lifts at 70 per cent, seven at 80 per cent, five at 85 per cent and five at 85 per cent. These lifts should be done with a medium to slow

rhythm. They supplement power and strength endurance.
3. Lifting at 60 to 70 per cent of maximum with six to ten repetitions in four to six sets. This type of lifting develops power and should be executed quickly. For example, the lifts should be undertaken in simple sets, such as four sets of ten repetitions at 70 per cent, and the bar should be moved really fast.

Weight training, to be done properly and safely, needs expert instruction. Physically immature athletes should not be loaded at these levels or physical damage will occur. With these athletes, strength training is best kept at the endurance level. Hopping and bounding with light loadings is also acceptable.

Many lifts relevant to the jumper and vaulter are shown in the BAAB strength training book. Eric McCalla is shown doing three lifting exercises relevant for jumpers in *Figs 97 to 105*.

Fig 98   Place the foot onto a stable bench.

Fig 99   Step up onto the bench, then step down, change legs and continue.
Remain stable at all times and do not put too much weight on the bar.

Fig 100 Power clean – a good starting position: head up, back flat and the bar pulled towards the shins.

Fig 101 Extend the legs from the starting position and do not pull with the arms until the legs are fully extended.

Fig 102 The receiving position: push the elbows high from this position.

Fig 103 The finishing position: from this position, let the bar come down to waist level. Then, keeping the back straight and flat, bend the knees and put the bar on the floor.

Fig 104   Front squat – start with the bar in this position. Note the bench in position
to show the lower extremity of the movement.

Fig 105   Squat until the buttocks touch the bench, then return to the starting
position.

Mobility

Suppleness work should be a daily under-taking for the jumper. General activities are followed by more specific jump ex-ercises. *Figs 80 to 89* show some specific jump exercises. The BAAB book *Mobility Training* gives many examples of general and specific exercises.

With both beginners and improvers, mobility exercises should be of the slow stretching type, without bouncing or fast stretching. A suggested regime is fifteen seconds of slow stretch followed by ten seconds of relaxation, with eight rep-etitions of each exercise chosen. When the athlete has acquired a good range of movement, he can then move on to ballistic exercises if he so wishes.

Fig 106 Mid-air position for the skip drill.

Multiple Jumps and Skip Drills

Most of the activities of the jumping decathlon can be used for developing jumping skill as well as specific strength. The loadings must be altered to develop either skill or specific strength.

Skip drills, where the athlete when skipping assumes the thigh parallel position in midskip as in *Fig 106*, are very useful. In doing these exercises, the athlete can also concentrate upon good body posture, the selected arm action and 'good reaching and pawing' technique.

EXAMPLES OF TRAINING SCHEDULES

These schedules are not meant to be definitive. Each athlete must work in his own situation at his own level. The follow-ing suggestions should be regarded as starting points. Discussion with experi-enced coaches and other athletes is also recommended.

Long Jumpers and Triple Jumpers

Complete Beginners

Assuming that the event has already been learned.

1. Jog two laps to warm up.
2. General mobility exercises.
3. Specific mobility exercises, centred upon the hip, hamstring, and lower back area.
4. Six jumps off a seven stride approach, for technique, particularly emphasising three equal phases, flat foot landings and good landing and take-off technique for

the triple jump and a fast take-off foot for the long jump.

5. Three jumps off an eleven stride approach. Observe to see if technique is held.

6. Acceleration runs over 60 metres × 6. Build speed for 20 metres, run quickly for 20 metres, then slow down over the next 20 metres.

Young Club Athletes

A. Training twice per week in winter.

Session one
1. Warm up by jogging.
2. Mobility exercises.
3. Eight skip drills, emphasising thigh parallel and good foot strike. Twelve ground contacts per repetition.
4. Twelve short approach jumps for technique.
5. Four × 120 metres sprint, with walk back recovery.
6. Warm down.

Session two
1. Warm up by jogging.
2. Mobility exercises.
3. Sprint drills.
4. Rhythm runs on the approach run (runway work should be done in winter when the search is for proper rhythm; accuracy comes in the competitive season).
5. Light bounding work emphasising light, quick strike action of the foot.
6. Warm down.

B. Training twice per week in summer.

Session one
1. Warm up by jogging.
2. Mobility exercises.
3. Four skip drills for technique; 12 ground contacts.

4. Jumping: 3 jumps off a 7 stride approach, 3 off 11 strides and once per fortnight 2 off a full approach. (If the athlete has foot or leg problems, care should be taken not to jump too much off longer runs.)
5. Rest.
6. Four × 60 metres at relaxed speed.
7. Warm down.

Session two
1. Warm up by jogging.
2. Mobility exercises.
3. Sprint drills.
4. Four rhythm runs on the runway.
5. Four accuracy runs. *Remember* – the athlete must take off to produce accuracy; a run-through without take-off does not produce accuracy.
6. Bounding activities, preferably light, but not too near to the competition.
7. Warm down.

Mature Club Athletes

A. Training four times per week in winter.

Session one
1. Warm up.
2. Mobility exercises.
3. Weight training – six exercises: bench press; seated press; power clean; hang snatch; front squat; step-ups onto bench.
4. Trunk stabilising exercises: sit-ups; back raises; side raises.
5. Warm down.

Session two
1. Warm up.
2. Mobility exercises.
3. Sprint drills plus rhythm runs × 4.
4. Jumping for technique – short approach.

Training

5. Rest.

6. Bounding: hop left leg; hop right leg; stepping; hop–hop–step–step. Twelve ground contacts × 4 sets. Walk back recovery between repetitions.

7. Warm down.

Session three

1. Warm up.

2. Mobility exercises.

3. Weight lifting as in session one.

4. Easy thirty minute run.

5. Warm down.

Session four

1. Warm up.

2. Mobility exercises.

3. Sprint drills.

4. Broken 150s × 6 (i.e. run hard for 60 metres, slow down for 30 metres and run hard again for 60 metres – walk back).

5. Rest.

6. Jumps specific circuit training.

7. Warm down.

B. Training four times per week in the summer.

Session one

1. Warm up.

2. Mobility exercises.

3. Weight lifting – similar exercises as winter, but executed faster with lighter weights.

4. Warm down.

Session two

1. Warm up.

2. Mobility exercises.

3. Sprint drills.

4. Four rhythm runs on runway. Four accuracy runs.

5. Short approach jumps for technique.

6. Warm down.

Session three

1. Warm up.

2. Mobility exercises.

3. Weight lifting: front squats – 4 sets of 10 at 60 per cent maximum, alternated with 5 hops and a jump × 4 into triple jump pit (2 off left foot, 2 off right foot) between each lifting set. Power cleans – 4 sets of 10 at 60 per cent alternated with 4 sets of 5 spring jumps, between each lifting set.

4. Six fast but relaxed runs over 40 metres. Long rest recovery.

5. Warm down.

Session four

1. Warm up.

2. Mobility exercises.

3. Two rhythm runs on runway. Six accuracy runs.

4. Short approach jumps for technique (and long approach jumps when necessary)

5. Six acceleration 60s.

Pole Vaulters

Complete Beginners

Assuming that the first stages of the event have already been learned.

1. Jog two laps to warm up.

2. General mobility exercises.

3. Specific mobility exercises for the shoulders, hips and hamstrings.

4. Swinging practices on the pole, planting and jumping into a long jump pit. Rehearse the correct hold on the pole and gain confidence in swinging on the pole. Do not hold the pole too high at first.

5. Ten vaults into the proper landing area off a nine stride approach run, aiming for: co-ordination of the plant and take-off; a

80

good take-off position, showing a high top hand and a good free leg position.

6. Six runs over the approach run to achieve the correct rhythm into an aggressive take-off.

7. Warm down.

Young Club Athletes

A. Training twice a week in winter.

Session one

1. Warm up, jogging two to four laps.
2. Mobility exercises.
3. Gymnastic exercises such as various types of handstand, backward roll to handstand, rope swinging and exercises on the parallel or high bar.
4. Four × 120 metres sprint at high speed with a brisk walk back recovery.
5. Warm down.

Session two

1. Warm up.
2. Mobility exercises.
3. Sprint drills.
4. Vaulting to improve an aspect of technique, particularly emphasising the plant and take-off.
5. Warm down.

B. Training twice a week in summer.

Session one

1. Warm up, jogging two to four laps.
2. Mobility exercises.
3. Gymnastic exercises, continuing from the winter session.
4. Vaulting for technique. Identify strengths and weaknesses and concentrate upon one technical point at a time from the approach run or plant and take-off, hang, rock back or bar clearance.
5. Warm down.

Session two

1. Warm up.
2. Mobility exercises.
3. Sprint drills.
4. Acceleration runs on the runway.
5. Accuracy runs on the runway.
6. Six vaults for runway speed, rhythm and good crisp take-offs.
7. Warm down.

Mature Club Athletes

A. Training four times per week in winter.

Session one

1. Warm up.
2. Mobility exercises.
3. Gymnastic exercises that include weight bearing on the arms, covering floor exercises and exercises on the parallel and high bars.
4. Trunk stabilising exercises: sit-ups; back raises; side raises.
5. Warm down.

Session two

1. Warm up.
2. Mobility exercises.
3. Sprint drills plus rhythm runs × 4.
4. Vaulting for technique – short approach.
5. Rest.
6. Bounding: hop left leg; hop right leg; stepping; hop–hop–step–step. Twelve ground contacts × 4 sets. Walk back recovery between repetitions.
7. Warm down.

Session three

1. Warm up.
2. Mobility exercises.
3. Weight lifting – six exercises: bench press; seated press; power clean; hang snatch; front squat; step-ups on bench.

Training

4. Easy thirty minute run.
5. Warm down.

Session four
1. Warm up.
2. Mobility exercises.
3. Sprint drills.
4. Broken 150s × 6 (i.e. run hard for 60 metres, slow down for 30 metres and run hard again for 60 metres – walk back).
5. Rest.
6. Vault specific circuit training, including exercises for the trunk and shoulders.
7. Warm down.

B. Training four times per week in the summer.

Session one
1. Warm up.
2. Mobility exercises.
3. Weight lifting – similar exercises as winter, but executed faster with lighter weights.
4. Warm down.

Session two
1. Warm up.
2. Mobility exercises.
3. Sprint drills.
4. Four rhythm runs on runway. Four accuracy runs.
5. Vaulting for technique.
6. Warm down.

Session three
1. Warm up.
2. Mobility exercises.
3. Weight lifting: front squats – 4 sets of 10 at 60 per cent maximum, alternated with 5 hops and a jump × 4 into triple jump pit (2 off left foot, 2 off right foot) between each lifting set. Power cleans – 4 sets of 10 at 60 per cent alternated with 4 sets of 5

spring jumps, between each lifting set.
4. Six fast but relaxed runs over 40 metres. Long rest recovery.
5. Warm down.

Session four
1. Warm up.
2. Mobility exercises.
3. Two rhythm runs on runway. Six accuracy runs.
4. Short approach vaults for technique (and long approach vaults when necessary).
5. Six acceleration 60s.
6. Warm down.

High Jumpers

Complete Beginners

Assuming that the event has already been learned.

1. Jog two laps to warm up.
2. General mobility exercises.
3. Specific mobility exercises, centred upon the hip, hamstring and lower back area.
4. Six jumps off a seven stride approach for technique, emphasising a high inside shoulder and an emphatic lift of the knee of the free leg at take-off. If this point is successfully undertaken, think also of lifting the head and shoulders as you leave the bar.
5. Three jumps off a full approach. Observe to see if technique is held.
6. Acceleration runs over 60 metres × 6. Build speed for 20 metres, run quickly for 20 metres, then slow down over the next 20 metres.
7. Warm down.

Young Club Athletes

A. Training twice per week in winter.

Session one
1. Warm up by jogging.
2. Mobility exercises.
3. Skip drills × 8, emphasising thigh parallel and the knee opposite the hip of the take-off leg. Twelve ground contacts per repetition.
4. Short approach jumps × 12 for technique.
5. Four × 80 metres sprint, with walk back recovery.
6. Warm down.

Session two
1. Warm up by jogging.
2. Mobility exercises.
3. Sprint drills and bar clearance drills.
4. Approach run practice, emphasising the change in body posture during the run and the change in speed into take-off.
5. Light bounding work emphasising light, quick strike action of the foot.
6. Warm down.

B. Training twice per week in summer.

Session one
1. Warm up by jogging.
2. Mobility exercises.
3. Skip drills × 4 for technique
4. Jumping: 6 jumps off a 7 stride approach, 6 off a full approach.
5. Rest.
6. Four × 60 metres at relaxed speed.
7. Warm down.

Session two
1. Warm up by jogging.
2. Mobility exercises.
3. Bar clearance drills.

4. Four approach runs on the high jump fan.
5. Six full jumps for a particular aspect of technique.
6. Bounding activities, preferably light, but not too near to the competition.
7. Warm down.

Mature Club Athletes

A. Training four times per week in winter.

Session one
1. Warm up.
2. Mobility exercises.
3. Weight training – six exercises: bench press; seated press; power clean; hang snatch; front squat; step-ups onto bench.
4. Trunk stabilising exercises: sit-ups; back raises; side raises.
5. Warm down.

Session two
1. Warm up.
2. Mobility exercises.
3. Approach run drills.
4. Jumping for technique – short approach.
5. Rest.
6. Bounding: hop left leg; hop right leg; stepping; hop–hop–step–step. Twelve ground contacts × 4 sets. Walk back recovery between repetitions.
7. Warm down.

Session three
1. Warm up.
2. Mobility exercises.
3. Weight lifting as in session one.
4. Easy thirty minute run.
5. Warm down.

Session four
1. Warm up.
2. Mobility exercises.

Training

3. Sprint drills.
4. Broken 150s × 6 (i.e. run hard for 60 metres, slow down for 30 metres and run hard again for 60 metres – walk back).
5. Rest.
6. Jumps specific circuit training.
7. Warm down.

B. Training four times per week in summer.

Session one
1. Warm up.
2. Mobility exercises.
3. Weight lifting – similar exercises as winter, but executed faster with lighter weights.
4. Warm down.

Session two
1. Warm up.
2. Mobility exercises.
3. Bar clearance drills.
4. Four rhythm runs on the fan.
5. Short approach jumps for technique.
6. Warm down.

Session three
1. Warm up.
2. Mobility exercises.
3. Weight lifting; front squats – 4 sets of 10 at 60 per cent maximum, alternated with 5 hops and a jump × 4 into triple jump pit (2 off left foot, 2 off right foot) between each lifting set. Power cleans – 4 sets of 10 at 60 per cent alternated with 4 sets of 5 spring jumps, between each lifting set.
4. Six fast but relaxed runs over 40 metres. Long rest recovery.
5. Warm down.

Session four
1. Warm up.

2. Mobility exercises.
3. Six rhythm runs on runway. Jumping and bar clearance drills.
4. Short approach jumps for technique (and long approach jumps when necessary).
5. Six acceleration 60s.
6. Warm down.

Warning

These schedules are neither exhaustive nor definitive. They are meant as a guide only. Essentially, training schedules should be set by the coach and athlete in the light of the athlete's ability, stage of development, state of fitness and facilities and time available. Please read the foregoing schedules to help you on your way to training schedules for *your* situation.

CONTROL TESTS FOR JUMPERS

Control tests are generally used to monitor the progress and the effectiveness of training. The ultimate test is the actual competitive performance. When tests are used, it must be remembered that they must show the following standards:

1. Validity – they must test what they set out to test.
2. Reliability – they should be capable of persistent repetition in any circumstances.
3. Objectivity – they should produce a consistent result irrespective of the person who is conducting the test.

Tests can be administered at any time of the competitive or training year, but it is usually best to decide which tests are to be incorporated into the training schedule at the beginning of the training year, with tests administered on a monthly basis to monitor progress. They can set out to test any of the following qualities.

Excellent – more than 70cm.
Good – 62 to 70cm.
Average – 54 to 62cm.
Fair – 45 to 54cm.
Poor – below 45cm.

Endurance

1. 1,000 metres run.
2. 5,000 metres run.

Speed

1. 40 metres sprint from a standing start. The stop-watch is started when the first foot strikes the ground and is stopped when the athlete crosses the finish line.
2. 60 metres sprint from blocks.
3. 100 metres sprint from blocks.
4. 200 metres sprint from blocks.

Strength

1. 100 per cent maximum in any one lift (not for physically immature athletes).
2. A six repetition maximum for any lift.
3. A ten repetition maximum for any lift.

Power exercises such as jump squats, power cleans, clean and jerk, step-ups onto a low bench or snatch could be tested under the strength heading.

Jumping Ability and Allied Strength

1. Sargent jump (*Figs 107 to 109*). The following classification will give club athletes some idea of the standard they should attain. The test is administered by going to stretch height with the fingertips. Then the athlete jumps and reaches as high as possible with the fingertips. The difference between stretch height and jump height is then measured.

Fig 107   A sargent jump – stretch to full fingertip height.

85

Training

Fig 108   Wet the finger and jump . . .

Fig 109   . . . to full stretch height. Note the
difference between stretch height
and jump height to give vertical
jump index.

Fig 110 A standing long jump – put the toes over the edge of the pit.

Fig 111 Take off from two feet and jump for distance.

Fig 112 Measure from the mark in the sand nearest to the take-off point to give the standing long jump index.

2. Standing long jump (*Figs 110 to 112*). Use the jumps decathlon table (*Fig 113*) for standards in this event.
3. Four hops and a jump into the sand pit, from a five stride approach.
4. Standing triple jump, plus all of the jumps shown in the jumps decathlon.
5. Standing back flip (*see Figs 28 to 31*).

Points	1 Stand Long Jump	2 Stand Triple Jump	3 2 Hops Step & Jump	4 2 Hops 2 Steps & Jump	5 2 Hops 2 Steps 2 Jumps	6 5 Spring Jumps	7 Stand 4 Hops & Jump	8 Run 4 Hops & Jump	9 25m Hop in secs	10 5 Stride Long Jump
100	3·73m	10·51m	13·00m	15·54m	19·15m	17·06m	17·67m	23·77m	2·07	7·28m
99	—	10·43m	12·90m	15·46m	18·99m	16·91m	17·52m	23·62m	—	—
98	3·65m	10·36m	12·80m	15·39m	18·84m	16·76m	17·37m	23·46m	2·08	—
97	—	10·28m	12·69m	15·31m	18·69m	16·61m	17·22m	23·31m	—	7·26m
96	3·58m	10·21m	12·59m	15·08m	18·54m	16·45m	17·06m	23·16m	3·00	—
95	—	10·13m	12·49m	15·01m	18·38m	16·40m	16·96m	23·01m	—	—
94	3·50m	10·05m	12·39m	14·88m	18·23m	16·25m	16·86m	22·85m	3·01	7·23m
93	—	9·98m	12·29m	14·78m	18·08m	16·15m	16·76m	22·70m	—	—
92	3·42m	9·90m	12·19m	14·68m	17·93m	16·00m	16·61m	22·55m	3·02	—
91	—	9·82m	12·09m	14·57m	17·77m	15·84m	16·45m	22·35m	—	7·21m
90	3·35m	9·75m	11·98m	14·47m	17·62m	15·79m	16·35m	21·99m	3·03	—
89	—	9·68m	11·88m	14·37m	17·47m	15·64m	16·25m	21·79m	—	—
88	3·27m	9·60m	11·78m	14·27m	17·32m	15·54m	16·15m	21·64m	3·04	7·18m
87	—	9·52m	11·68m	14·17m	17·17m	15·39m	16·00m	21·48m	—	—
86	3·20m	9·44m	11·58m	14·07m	17·01m	15·23m	15·84m	21·33m	3·05	—
85	—	9·37m	11·48m	13·96m	16·91m	15·18m	15·74m	21·18m	—	7·16m
84	3·12m	9·29m	11·37m	13·86m	16·76m	15·03m	15·64m	21·03m	3·06	—
83	—	9·22m	11·27m	13·76m	16·66m	14·93m	15·54m	20·80m	3·07	7·13m
82	3·04m	9·14m	11·17m	13·66m	16·50m	14·83m	15·44m	20·65m	3·08	—
81	—	9·06m	11·07m	13·56m	16·35m	14·68m	15·34m	20·42m	3·09	7·11m
80	2·97m	8·99m	10·97m	13·46m	16·20m	14·57m	15·23m	20·26m	4·00	—
79	—	8·91m	10·87m	13·36m	16·10m	14·42m	15·08m	20·11m	4·02	7·08m
78	2·89m	8·83m	10·76m	13·25m	16·00m	14·32m	14·93m	19·96m	4·03	—
77	—	8·76m	10·66m	13·15m	15·84m	14·22m	14·83m	19·81m	4·04	7·06m
76	2·81m	8·68m	10·56m	13·05m	15·69m	14·07m	14·73m	19·58m	4·05	7·03m
75	—	8·61m	10·46m	12·95m	15·54m	13·96m	14·63m	19·43m	4·06	7·01m
74	2·74m	8·53m	10·36m	12·85m	15·39m	13·86m	14·47m	19·20m	4·07	6·95m
73	2·69m	8·45m	10·26m	12·75m	15·23m	13·71m	14·32m	19·04m	4·08	6·90m
72	2·66m	8·38m	10·15m	12·64m	15·13m	13·61m	14·22m	18·89m	4·09	6·85m
71	2·64m	8·30m	10·05m	12·49m	15·03m	13·51m	14·12m	18·74m	5·00	6·80m
70	2·61m	8·22m	9·95m	12·42m	14·88m	13·41m	14·02m	18·59m	5·01	6·75m
69	2·59m	8·15m	9·85m	12·34m	14·73m	13·25m	13·86m	18·44m	5·02	6·70m
68	2·56m	8·07m	9·75m	12·19m	14·63m	13·10m	13·71m	18·28m	5·04	6·62m
67	2·53m	8·00m	9·65m	12·09m	14·47m	13·00m	13·61m	18·13m	5·05	6·55m
66	2·51m	7·92m	9·55m	11·98m	14·32m	12·90m	13·51m	17·98m	5·06	6·47m
65	2·48m	7·84m	9·44m	11·88m	14·22m	12·80m	13·41m	17·75m	5·07	6·40m
64	2·46m	7·77m	9·34m	11·78m	14·07m	12·69m	13·30m	17·60m	5·08	6·32m
63	2·43m	7·69m	9·24m	11·68m	13·96m	12·59m	13·20m	17·37m	5·09	6·24m
62	2·41m	7·61m	9·14m	11·58m	13·81m	12·49m	13·10m	17·22m	6·00	6·17m
61	2·38m	7·54m	9·04m	11·48m	13·71m	12·34m	12·95m	17·06m	6·01	6·09m
60	2·36m	7·46m	8·94m	11·37m	13·56m	12·19m	12·80m	16·91m	6·02	6·01m
59	2·33m	7·39m	8·83m	11·27m	13·41m	12·03m	12·64m	16·76m	6·03	5·94m
58	2·31m	7·31m	8·73m	11·17m	13·25m	11·88m	12·49m	16·53m	6·05	5·86m
57	2·28m	7·23m	8·63m	11·07m	13·10m	11·78m	12·39m	16·38m	6·06	5·79m
56	2·26m	7·16m	8·53m	10·97m	12·95m	11·68m	12·29m	16·15m	6·07	5·71m
55	2·23m	7·08m	8·45m	10·87m	12·60m	11·58m	12·19m	16·00m	6·08	5·63m
54	2·20m	7·01m	8·38m	10·76m	12·54m	11·48m	12·09m	15·84m	6·09	5·56m
53	2·18m	6·91m	8·30m	10·66m	12·49m	11·37m	11·98m	15·69m	7·00	5·48m
52	2·15m	6·85m	8·22m	10·56m	12·34m	11·27m	11·58m	15·54m	7·01	5·41m
51	2·13m	6·78m	8·15m	10·46m	12·19m	11·17m	11·42m	15·39m	7·02	5·33m
50	2·10m	6·70m	8·07m	10·36m	12·01m	11·07m	11·27m	15·21m	7·03	5·25m

Fig 113   The jumps decathlon scoring table.

Jumping Decathlon (Fig 113)

The tables shown in Fig 113 were compiled graphically and extended to cover the lower ability ranges. Approximations were made in some cases to prevent fractions of a centimetre from coming in to the scale. In all events except the five stride long jump the mean was taken from test results obtained from non-specialist

Points	1 Stand Long Jump	2 Stand Triple Jump	3 2 Hops Step & Jump	4 2 Hops 2 Steps & Jump	5 2 Hops 2 Steps 2 Jumps	6 5 Spring Jumps	7 Stand 4 Hops & Jump	8 Run 4 Hops & Jump	9 25m Hop in secs	10 5 Stride Long Jump
49	2·08m	6·62m	8·00m	10·26m	11·88m	10·97m	11·17m	15·08m	7·04	5·18m
48	2·05m	6·55m	7·92m	10·15m	11·73m	10·87m	11·07m	14·93m	—	5·13m
47	2·03m	6·47m	7·84m	10·05m	11·58m	10·76m	10·97m	14·78m	7·05	5·07m
46	2·00m	6·40m	7·77m	9·95m	11·42m	10·66m	10·82m	14·63m	—	5·02m
45	1·98m	6·32m	7·69m	9·85m	11·27m	10·56m	10·66m	14·47m	7·07	4·97m
44	1·95m	6·24m	7·61m	9·75m	11·17m	10·46m	10·51m	14·32m	—	4·92m
43	1·93m	6·17m	7·54m	9·65m	11·07m	10·36m	10·36m	14·17m	7·08	4·87m
42	1·90m	6·09m	7·46m	9·55m	10·97m	10·26m	10·21m	14·02m	—	4·82m
41	1·87m	6·01m	7·39m	9·44m	10·87m	10·15m	10·05m	13·86m	7·09	4·77m
40	1·85m	5·94m	7·31m	9·34m	10·76m	10·05m	9·90m	13·71m	—	4·72m
39	1·82m	5·86m	7·23m	9·24m	10·66m	9·95m	9·75m	13·56m	8·00	4·67m
38	1·80m	5·79m	7·16m	9·14m	10·56m	9·85m	9·60m	13·41m	—	4·62m
37	1·77m	5·71m	7·08m	9·04m	10·46m	9·75m	9·44m	13·25m	8·01	4·57m
36	1·75m	5·63m	7·01m	8·94m	10·36m	9·65m	9·34m	13·10m	—	4·52m
35	1·72m	5·56m	6·93m	8·83m	10·26m	9·55m	9·24m	12·95m	8·02	4·47m
34	1·70m	5·48m	6·85m	8·73m	10·15m	9·44m	9·14m	12·80m	—	4·41m
33	1·67m	5·41m	6·78m	8·63m	10·05m	9·34m	9·04m	12·64m	8·03	4·36m
32	1·65m	5·33m	6·70m	8·53m	9·95m	9·24m	8·94m	12·49m	—	4·31m
31	1·62m	5·25m	6·62m	8·43m	9·85m	9·14m	8·83m	12·34m	8·04	4·26m
30	1·60m	5·18m	6·55m	8·33m	9·75m	9·04m	8·73m	12·19m	—	4·21m
29	1·57m	5·10m	6·47m	8·22m	9·65m	8·94m	8·63m	12·03m	8·05	4·16m
28	1·54m	5·02m	6·40m	8·12m	9·55m	8·83m	8·53m	11·88m	—	4·11m
27	1·52m	4·95m	6·32m	8·02m	9·44m	8·73m	8·43m	11·73m	8·06	4·06m
26	1·49m	4·87m	6·24m	7·92m	9·34m	8·63m	8·33m	11·58m	—	4·01m
25	1·47m	4·80m	6·17m	7·82m	9·24m	8·53m	8·22m	11·42m	8·07	3·96m
24	1·44m	4·72m	6·09m	7·72m	9·14m	8·43m	8·12m	11·27m	—	3·91m
23	1·42m	4·64m	5·99m	7·61m	9·04m	8·33m	8·02m	11·12m	—	3·86m
22	1·39m	4·57m	5·89m	7·51m	8·94m	8·22m	7·92m	10·97m	8·09	3·80m
21	1·37m	4·49m	5·79m	7·41m	8·83m	8·12m	7·82m	10·82m	—	3·75m
20	1·34m	4·41m	5·68m	7·31m	8·73m	8·02m	7·72m	10·66m	—	3·70m
19	1·29m	4·26m	5·58m	7·21m	8·63m	7·92m	7·61m	10·51m	9·00	3·65m
18	1·26m	4·19m	5·48m	7·11m	8·53m	7·82m	7·51m	10·36m	—	3·60m
17	1·24m	4·11m	5·38m	7·01m	8·43m	7·72m	7·41m	10·21m	—	3·55m
16	1·21m	4·03m	5·28m	6·90m	8·33m	7·61m	7·31m	10·05m	9·01	3·50m
15	1·19m	3·96m	5·18m	6·80m	8·22m	7·51m	7·21m	9·90m	—	3·45m
14	1·16m	3·88m	5·07m	6·70m	8·12m	7·41m	7·11m	9·75m	—	3·40m
13	1·14m	3·80m	4·97m	6·60m	8·02m	7·31m	7·01m	9·60m	9·02	3·35m
12	1·11m	3·73m	4·87m	6·50m	7·92m	7·21m	6·90m	9·44m	—	3·25m
11	1·09m	3·65m	4·77m	6·40m	7·82m	7·11m	6·80m	9·29m	—	3·14m
10	1·06m	3·58m	4·67m	6·29m	7·72m	7·01m	6·70m	9·14m	9·03	3·04m
9	1·04m	3·50m	4·57m	6·19m	7·61m	6·90m	6·60m	8·99m	—	2·94m
8	1·01m	3·42m	4·47m	6·09m	7·51m	6·80m	6·50m	8·83m	—	2·84m
7	0·99m	3·35m	4·36m	5·99m	7·41m	6·70m	6·40m	8·68m	9·04	2·74m
6	0·96m	3·27m	4·26m	5·89m	7·31m	6·60m	6·29m	8·53m	—	2·64m
5	0·93m	3·20m	4·16m	5·79m	7·21m	6·50m	6·19m	8·38m	—	2·53m
4	0·91m	3·12m	4·06m	5·68m	7·11m	6·40m	6·09m	8·22m	9·05	2·43m
3	0·88m	3·04m	3·96m	5·58m	7·01m	6·29m	5·99m	8·07m	—	2·33m
2	0·86m	2·97m	3·86m	5·48m	6·90m	6·19m	5·89m	7·92m	—	2·23m
1	0·60m	2·89m	3·75m	5·38m	6·70m	6·09m	5·79m	7·77m	9·06	2·13m

groups at Young Athletes Courses. In most cases the top mark is that of the approximate world record for the event, mainly set by professional jumpers, of the late nineteenth century. The mean for the five stride long jump is taken from tests given to specialist jumpers. Hence the tables cannot be used to compare one leaping event with another. Their main aim is to encourage leaping and bounding as an enjoyable means of training for other events with a little direct and indirect competition as an added incentive. The events are not necessarily listed in the best order.

1. Standing broad jump. Both feet together; arms can be used to aid lift. Measurement to nearest point of contact.
2. Standing triple. Take-off foot to remain in flat contact with the ground, although free swinging of non-contact leg can be used. The same rule is applied to the other three hop, step and jump combinations.
3. Two hops, two steps, two jumps. The second of the two jumps is made from a two foot take-off.
4. Five spring jumps. Five successive two foot bounds. The feet must be kept together and the movement must be continuous.
5. Standing four hops and a jump. Start as for standing triple. Tables compiled for dominant leg.
6. Running four hops and a jump. Length of run unlimited.
7. Twenty-five metre hop. From standing position. Tables compiled for dominant leg, although the mean of left and right should be the recorded performance.
8. Five stride long jump. Normal jumping rules, except that the run is limited to five strides.

Most of the events are educable and performance can improve with training. All ten events, allowing two or three successful attempts at each, is a good single training session for any power-thirsty athlete.

Mobility

Mobility can be tested in a number of ways, but these often need specialised and expensive equipment. Subjective scrutiny by the coach is very effective.

8 Summary of Jumping Rules

Separate rule books are issued by the International Amateur Athletic Federation, the Amateur Athletic Association and the Women's Amateur Athletic Association. Ideally, athletes should carry a relevant rule book with them all the time. The following rules are only summaries and rule books must be referred to for the exact wording of rules.

Competition Procedures

Athletes should travel to the venue of their event so that they reach there in good time. They will be required to report their presence to the organisers and collect competition numbers and programmes. Sufficient time must be allowed to report to the competition area, usually some thirty minutes before the event is due to start. Warming-up is done before this, with final run-up checks and practice jumps done in the thirty minutes before the event begins.

Distance Jumps

In jumps for distance athletes are given up to six jumps. In large competitions they will be given three jumps, with the best eight competitors having a further three jumps. In even larger competitions there will be two 'pools' of competitors, with those who achieve a previously published qualifying standard proceeding to the final. It should be noted that qualifying jumps in the pool will not be counted in the final.

Where there is a tie, the second best mark will be taken into account. If there is still a tie the third best mark will be taken into account, and so on, until the tie is resolved.

A no jump will be given if the athlete takes off beyond the scratch line, which is the edge of the board nearest the sand. A plasticine no jump indicator is usually present. If the athlete's foot marks this indicator, it is a no jump. The jump is measured from the nearest mark to the scratch line made in the sand by the athlete. It is measured from that mark, at right angles to the scratch line. If the athlete lands in the sand and then falls backwards out of the pit, so that he lands behind the mark made in the pit, this also is a no jump.

Height Jumps

In jumps for height, athletes will be disqualified from further participation if they have three consecutive failures at any height.

A high jumper fails if he passes the plane of the uprights – inside or outside of these – without clearing the bar. He also fails if he takes off from two feet.

A high jumper can commence jumping at any height above the minimum set by the judges and can then continue at his discretion at any subsequent height. This means that the athlete can forego second and third jumps at a particular height and

Summary of Jumping Rules

still jump at a subsequent height. The athlete can place marks to assist him in his run-up and take-off. If an athlete wins a competition, he can continue jumping until he has forfeited his right to jump – i.e. until he has had three consecutive failures.

In pole vault, the vaulter fails if he leaves the ground but does not clear the bar, if he knocks off the bar with his body or the pole or lets his pole go past the end of the planting box and touches the ground or landing area beyond. Generally, the other rules are as for the high jump.

Vaulting poles are now very sophisticated and expensive and attention should be paid to their care. During competition, the gripping area can be bound with no more than two layers of tape. Athletes usually have to report to the competition area before the competition, so that the judges can inspect their poles. Athletes may use a sticky substance, usually Venice turpentine, on their hands during the competition.

These are the main rules for the jumping events, together with some tips for the competition itself. To become totally conversant with the rules, buy a rule book. Addresses from which they can be purchased appear at the back of this book.

Appendix

BRITISH RECORDS 1860–1985

MEN

High Jump

1.70m	R. H. L. Burton	1860
1.71m	Tom Mitchell	1864
1.72m	J. H. T. Roupell	1866
1.75m	T. G. Little	1866
1.75m	J. H. T.Roupell	1866
1.75m	T. G. Little	1867
1.76m	R. J. C. Mitchell	1871
1.78m	Tom Davin (Ireland)	1873
1.80m	Marshall Brooks	1874
1.80m	M. G. Glazebrook	1875
1.83m	Marshall Brooks	1876
1.89m	Marshall Brooks	1876
1.90m	Patrick Davin (Ireland)	1880
1.90m	George Rowdon	1889
1.90m	Murty O'Brien (Ireland)	1893
1.91m	James Ryan (Ireland)	1893
1.92m	James Ryan	1895
1.94m	James Ryan	1895
1.95m	Pat Leahy (Ireland)	1898
1.96m	Tim Carroll (Ireland)	1913
1.96m	Howard Baker	1921
1.96m	Alan Patterson	1946
1.97m	Alan Patterson	1946
2.00m	Alan Patterson	1946
2.02m	Alan Patterson	1947
2.02m	Peter Wells	1954
2.05m	Crawford Fairbrother	1959
2.05m	Gordon Miller	1960
2.06m	Crawford Fairbrother	1961
2.06m	Crawford Fairbrother	1962
2.07m	Gordon Miller	1964
2.08m	Gordon Miller	1964
2.08m	Mike Campbell	1971
2.08m	Dave Livesey	1972
2.10m	Alan Lerwill	1973
2.11m	Gordon Boreham	1974
2.12m	Mike Butterfield	1975
2.14m	Mike Butterfield	1975
2.14m	Angus Mckenzie	1975
2.15m	Brian Burgess	1976
2.17m	Mark Naylor	1978
2.17m	Brian Burgess	1978
2.20m	Brian Burgess	1978
2.20m	Mark Naylor	1980
2.22m	Mark Naylor	1980
2.24m	Mark Naylor	1980
2.25m	Geoff Parsons	1983
2.26m	Geoff Parsons	1984

Long Jump

6.37m	C. F. Buller	1862
6.39m	A. C. Tosswill	1868
6.50m	A. C. Tosswill	1866
6.75m	A. C. Tosswill	1869
6.85m	Jenner Davies	1872
6.97m	Jenner Davies	1874
7.05m	John Lane (Ireland)	1874
7.06m	Patrick Davin (Ireland)	1883
7.06m	Patrick Davin (Ireland)	1883
7.08m	John Purcell (Ireland)	1886
7.14m	Charles Fry	1892
7.17m	Charles Fry	1893
7.21m	J. J. Mooney (Ireland)	1894
7.24m	William Newburn (Ireland)	1898
7.33m	William Newburn (Ireland)	1898
7.51m	Peter O'Connor (Ireland)	1900

Appendix

7.54m	Peter O'Connor (Ireland)	1901
7.60m	Peter O'Connor (Ireland)	1901
7.61m	Peter O'Connor (Ireland)	1901
7.63m	John Howell	1960
7.72m	Lynn Davies	1962
7.72m	John Morbey	1963
7.72m	John Morbey	1964
8.01m	Lynn Davies	1964
8.02m	Lynn Davies	1964
8.07m	Lynn Davies	1964
8.13m	Lynn Davies	1966
8.18m	Lynn Davies	1966
8.23m	Lynn Davies	1968

Triple Jump

14.50m	Dan Shanahan (Ireland)	1886
14.70m	John Purcell (Ireland)	1887
14.91m	Tim Ahearne (Ireland)	1908
15.28m	Ken Wilmshurst	1954
15.44m	Ken Wilmshurst	1955
15.60m	Ken Wilmshurst	1956
15.65m	Fred Alsop	1960
15.66m	Fred Alsop	1960
15.78m	Fred Alsop	1961
16.03m	Fred Alsop	1962
16.13m	Fred Alsop	1964
16.46m	Fred Alsop	1964
16.52m	Aston Moore	1976
16.68m	Aston Moore	1978
16.76m	Keith Connor	1978
17.16m	Keith Connor	1980
17.57m	Keith Connor	1982

Pole Vault

Pole 'swarming' or 'climbing' technique.

3.05m	J. Wheeler	1866
3.05m	A. Lubbock	1868
3.21m	R. J. C. Mitchell	1868
3.22m	Edwin Woodburn	1873

3.22m	W. Kelsey	1873
3.22m	J. Wigful	1883
3.22m	Edwin Woodburn	1874
3.22m	J. Wigful	1875
3.26m	G. W. Gaskin	1876
3.32m	G. W. Gaskin	1876
3.38m	Edwin Woodburn	1876
3.38m	H. E. Kayll	1877
3.42m	Tom Ray	1879
3.43m	Tom Ray	1881
3.45m	Tom Ray	1882
3.46m	Tom Ray	1883
3.48m	Tom Ray	1885
3.48m	Tom Ray	1886
3.50m	Tom Ray	1887
3.52m	Tom Ray	1887
3.53m	E. L. Stones	1888
3.57m	Tom Ray	1888
3.57m	E. L. Stones	1889
3.58m	Richard Dickinson	1891

Conventional techique – heights cleared under present day rules.

3.61m	L. T. Bond	1928
3.69m	L. T. Bond	1930
3.77m	L. T. Bond	1930
3.81m	L. T. Bond	1930
3.85m	L. T. Bond	1931
3.86m	Richard Webster	1936
3.88m	Richard Webster	1936
3.90m	Richard Webster	1936
4.00m	Richard Webster	1936
4.11m	Norman Gregor	1951
4.11m	Geoff Elliott	1952
4.15m	Geoff Elliott	1952
4.16m	Geoff Elliott	1953
4.19m	Geoff Elliott	1953
4.26m	Geoff Elliott	1954
4.30m	Geoff Elliott	1954
4.30m	Geoff Elliott	1957
4.30m	Geoff Elliott	1958

4.30m	Geoff Elliott	1959
4.32m	Rex Porter	1963
4.37m	Trevor Burton	1963
4.39m	Rex Porter	1963
4.40m	David Stevenson	1963
4.41m	David Stevenson	1963
4.42m	David Stevenson	1963
4.43m	Trevor Burton	1964
4.46m	Trevor Burton	1964
4.57m	Trevor Burton	1964
4.60m	David Stevenson	1964
4.61m	David Stevenson	1964
4.65m	David Stevenson	1966
4.67m	David Stevenson	1966
4.72m	Mike Bull	1966
4.80m	Mike Bull	1967
4.94m	Mike Bull	1968
5.03m	Mike Bull	1968
5.07m	Mike Bull	1968
5.10m	Mike Bull	1970
5.11m	Mike Bull	1972
5.20m	Mike Bull	1972
5.21m	Mike Bull	1972
5.25m	Mike Bull	1973
5.29m	Brian Hooper	1976
5.30m	Brian Hooper	1976
5.31m	Brian Hooper	1976
5.32m	Brian Hooper	1976
5.32m	Brian Hooper	1977
5.37m	Brian Hooper	1977
5.40m	Brian Hooper	1977
5.41m	Brian Hooper	1978
5.42m	Brian Hooper	1978
5.45m	Brian Hooper	1980
5.50m	Brian Hooper	1980
5.51m	Brian Hooper	1980
5.52m	Keith Stock	1980
5.54m	Brian Hooper	1980
5.55m	Keith Stock	1980
5.56m	Brian Hooper	1980
5.57m	Keith Stock	1980
5.58m	Brian Hooper	1980
5.59m	Brian Hooper	1980

5.60m	Keith Stock	1981
5.65m	Keith Stock	1981

WOMEN

High Jump

1.39m	Hilda Hatt	1921
1.45m	Hilda Hatt	1922
1.46m	Ivy Lowman	1922
1.47m	Ivy Lowman	1923
1.48m	Sophia Elliott-Lynn	1923
1.48m	Ivy Lowman	1924
1.51m	Phyllis Green	1925
1.52m	Phyllis Green	1925
1.55m	Phyllis Green	1926
1.57m	Phyllis Green	1927
1.58m	Phyllis Green	1927
1.61m	Mary Milne	1935
1.65m	Dorothy Odham (Tyler)	1936
1.66m	Dorothy Odham (Tyler)	1939
1.68m	Dorothy Odham (Tyler)	1948
1.69m	Sheila Lerwill	1950
1.71m	Sheila Lerwill	1951
1.74m	Thelma Hopkins	1956
1.75m	Francis Slaap	1964
1.76m	Francis Slaap	1964
1.76m	Barbara Lawton	1964
1.76m	Linda Hedmark	1969
1.78m	Barbara Lawton	1969
1.79m	Linda Hedmark	1969
1.79m	Barbara Lawton	1970
1.83m	Linda Hedmark	1971
1.85m	Barbara Lawton	1971
1.85m	Barbara Lawton	1972
1.86m	Barbara Lawton	1972
1.87m	Barbara Lawton	1973
1.87m	Moira Maguire	1980
1.88m	Louise Miller	1980
1.90m	Louise Miller	1980
1.92m	Louise Miller	1980
1.94m	Lousie Miller	1980
1.95m	Diana Davies	1982

Long Jump

5.05m	Mary Lines	1922
5.17m	Mary Lines	1924
5.24m	Phyllis Green	1925
5.48m	Muriel Gunn	1926
5.60m	Muriel Gunn	1927
5.68m	Muriel Gunn	1928
5.78m	Muriel Gunn	1929
5.80m	Muriel Gunn	1930
5.85m	Muriel Gunn	1930
5.92m	Shirley Cawley	1952
6.10m	Jean Desforges	1953
6.14m	Sheila Hoskin	1956
6.20m	Mary Rand	1959
6.27m	Mary Rand	1960
6.33m	Mary Rand	1960
6.35m	Mary Rand	1963
6.44m	Mary Rand	1963
6.58m	Mary Rand	1964
6.76m	Mary Rand	1964
6.90m	Beverly Kinch	1983

WORLD RECORDS 1901–1985

MEN

Long Jump

7.61m	Peter O'Connor	GBR	1901
7.69m	Edward Gourdin	USA	1921
7.76m	Robert LeGendre	USA	1924
7.89m	William de Hart Hubbard	USA	1925
7.90m	Edward Hamm	USA	1928
7.93m	Sylvio Cator	HAITI	1928
7.98m	Chuhei Nambu	JAP	1931
8.13m	Jesse Owens	USA	1935
8.21m	Ralph Boston	USA	1960
8.24m	Ralph Boston	USA	1961
8.28m	Ralph Boston	USA	1962
8.31m	Igor Ter-Ovanesyan	URS	1962
8.31m	Ralph Boston	USA	1964
8.34m	Ralph Boston	USA	1964
8.35m	Ralph Boston	USA	1965
8.35m	Igor Ter-Ovanesyan	URS	1967
8.90m	Bob Beamon	USA	1968

Triple Jump

15.52m	Daniel Ahearn	USA	1911
15.52m	Anthony Winter	AUS	1924
15.58m	Mikio Oda	JAP	1931
15.72m	Chuhei Nambu	JAP	1932
15.78m	Jack Metcalfe	AUS	1935
16.00m	Naoto Tajima	JAP	1936
16.00m	Adhemar da Silva	BRA	1950
16.01m	Adhemar da Silva	BRA	1951
16.12m	Adhemar da Silva	BRA	1952
16.22m	Adhemar da Silva	BRA	1952
16.23m	Leonid Scherbakov	URS	1953
16.56m	Adhemar da Silva	BRA	1955
16.59m	Oleg Rhyakovsky	URS	1958
16.70m	Oleg Feyedoseyev	URS	1959
17.03m	Jozef Schmidt	POL	1960
17.10m	Giuseppe Gentile	ITA	1968
17.22m	Giuseppe Gentile	ITA	1968
17.23m	Viktor Saneyev	URS	1968
17.27m	Nelson Prudencio	BRA	1968
17.39m	Viktor Saneyev	URS	1968
17.40m	Pedro Perez Duenas	CUB	1971
17.44m	Viktor Saneyev	URS	1972
17.89m	Joao de Oliveira	BRA	1975
17.97m	Willie Banks	USA	1985

High Jump

2.00m	George Horine	USA	1912
2.01m	Edward Beeson	USA	1914
2.03m	Harold Osborn	USA	1924
2.04m	Walter Marty	USA	1933
2.06m	Walter Marty	USA	1934

2.07m	Cornelius Johnson	USA	1936
2.07m	David Albritton	USA	1936
2.09m	Mel Walker	USA	1937
2.11m	Lester Steers	USA	1941
2.12m	Walter Davies	USA	1953
2.15m	Charles Dumas	USA	1956
2.16m	Yuriy Styepanov	URS	1957
2.17m	John Thomas	USA	1960
2.18m	John Thomas	USA	1960
2.22m	John Thomas	USA	1960
2.23m	Valeriy Brumel	URS	1961
2.24m	Valeriy Brumel	URS	1961
2.25m	Valeriy Brumel	URS	1961
2.26m	Valeriy Brumel	URS	1962
2.27m	Valeriy Brumel	URS	1962
2.28m	Valeriy Brumel	URS	1963
2.29m	Patrick Matzdorf	USA	1971
2.30m	Dwight Stones	USA	1973
2.31m	Dwight Stones	USA	1976
2.32m	Dwight Stones	USA	1976
2.33m	Vladimir Yaschchenko	URS	1977
2.34m	Vladimir Yaschchenko	URS	1978
2.35m	Jacek Wszola	POL	1980
2.35m	Dietmar Moegenburg	FRG	1980
2.36m	Gerd Wessig	GDR	1980
2.37m	Jianhua Zhu	PRC	1983
2.38m	Jianhua Zhu	PRC	1983
2.39m	Jianhua Zhu	PRC	1984
2.40m	Rudolf Povarnitsin	URS	1985
2.41m	Igor Paklin	URS	1985

Pole Vault

4.02m	Marc Wright	USA	1912
4.09m	Frank Foss	USA	1920
4.12m	Charles Hoff	NOR	1922
4.21m	Charles Hoff	NOR	1923
4.23m	Charles Hoff	NOR	1925
4.25m	Charles Hoff	NOR	1925
4.27m	Sabin Carr	USA	1927
4.30m	Lee Barnes	USA	1928
4.37m	Bill Graber	USA	1932
4.39m	Keith Brown	USA	1935
4.43m	George Varoff	USA	1936

4.54m	Bill Sefton	USA	1937
4.54m	Earle Meadows	USA	1937
4.60m	Cornelius Warmerdam	USA	1940
4.72m	Cornelius Warmerdam	USA	1941
4.77m	Cornelius Warmerdam	USA	1942
4.78m	Bob Gutowski	USA	1957
4.80m	Don Bragg	USA	1960
4.83m	George Davies	USA	1961
4.89m	John Uelses	USA	1962
4.93m	David Tork	USA	1962
4.94m	Pentti Nikula	FIN	1962
5.00m	Brian Sternberg	USA	1963
5.08m	Brian Sternberg	USA	1963
5.13m	John Pennel	USA	1963
5.20m	John Pennel	USA	1963
5.23m	Fred Hansen	USA	1964
5.28m	Fred Hansen	USA	1964
5.32m	Bob Seagren	USA	1966
5.34m	John Pennel	USA	1966
5.36m	Bob Seagren	USA	1967
5.38m	Paul Wilson	USA	1967
5.41m	Bob Seagren	USA	1968
5.44m	John Pennel	USA	1969
5.45m	Wolfgang Nordwig	GDR	1970
5.46m	Wolfgang Nordwig	GDR	1970
5.49m	Christos Papanicolaou	GRE	1970
5.51m	Kjell Isaksson	SWE	1972
5.54m	Kjell Isaksson	SWE	1972
5.55m	Kjell Isaksson	SWE	1972
5.63m	Bob Seagren	USA	1972
5.65m	Dave Roberts	USA	1975
5.67m	Earl Bell	USA	1976
5.70m	Dave Roberts	USA	1976
5.72m	Wladyslaw Kozakiewicz	POL	1980
5.75m	Thierry Vigneron	FRA	1980
5.75m	Thierry Vigneron	FRA	1980
5.77m	Philippe Houvion	FRA	1980
5.78m	Wladyslaw Kozakiewicz	POL	1980
5.80m	Thierry Vigneron	FRA	1981
5.81m	Vladimir Poliakov	URS	1981
5.82m	Pierre Quinon	FRA	1983
5.83m	Thierry Vigneron	FRA	1983

5.85m	Sergei Bubka	URS	1984
5.88m	Sergei Bubka	URS	1984
5.90m	Sergei Bubka	URS	1984
5.91m	Thierry Vigneron	FRA	1984
5.94m	Sergei Bubka	URS	1984
6.00m	Sergei Bubka	URS	1985

WOMEN

High Jump

1.65m	Jean Shiley	USA	1932
1.65m	Mildred Didrikson	USA	1932
1.66m	Dorothy Odam	GBR	1939
1.66m	Esther van Heerden	RFA	1941
1.66m	Ilsebill Pfenning	SUI	1941
1.71m	Fanny Blankers-Koen	HOL	1943
1.72m	Sheila Lerwill	GBR	1951
1.73m	Aleksandra Chudina	URS	1954
1.74m	Thelma Hopkins	GBR	1956
1.75m	Iolanda Balas	ROM	1956
1.76m	Mildred McDaniel	USA	1956
1.76m	Iolanda Balas	ROM	1957
1.77m	Cheng Feng-Jung	PRC	1957
1.78m	Iolanda Balas	ROM	1958
1.80m	Iolanda Balas	ROM	1958
1.81m	Iolanda Balas	ROM	1958
1.82m	Iolanda Balas	ROM	1958
1.83m	Iolanda Balas	ROM	1958
1.84m	Iolanda Balas	ROM	1959
1.85m	Iolanda Balas	ROM	1960
1.86m	Iolanda Balas	ROM	1960
1.87m	Iolanda Balas	ROM	1961
1.88m	Iolanda Balas	ROM	1961
1.90m	Iolanda Balas	ROM	1961
1.91m	Iolanda Balas	ROM	1961
1.92m	Ilona Gusenbauer	AUT	1971
1.92m	Ulrike Meyfarth	FRG	1972
1.94m	Jordanka Blagoyeva	BUL	1972

1.94m	Rosemarie Witschas	GDR	1974
1.95m	Rosemarie Witschas	GDR	1974
1.96m	Rosemarie Ackermann	GDR	1976
1.96m	Rosemarie Ackermann	GDR	1977
1.97m	Rosemarie Ackermann	GDR	1977
2.00m	Rosemarie Ackermann	GDR	1977
2.01m	Sara Simeoni	ITA	1978
2.02m	Ulrike Meyfarth	FRG	1982
2.03m	Ulrike Meyfarth	FRG	1983
2.03m	Tamara Bykova	URS	1983
2.04m	Tamara Bykova	URS	1983
2.07m	Lyudmila Andonova	BUL	1984

Long Jump

5.98m	Kinue Hitomi	JAP	1928
6.12m	Christel Schulz	FRG	1939
6.25m	Fanny Blankers-Koen	HOL	1943
6.28m	Yvette Williams	NZL	1954
6.28m	Galina Vinogradova	URS	1955
6.31m	Galina Vinogradova	URS	1955
6.35m	Elzbieta Kresinska	POL	1956
6.40m	Hildrun Klaus	GDR	1960
6.42m	Hildrun Klaus	GDR	1961
6.48m	Tatyana Shchelkanova	URS	1961
6.53m	Tatyana Shchelkanova	URS	1962
6.70m	Tatyana Shchelkanova	URS	1964
6.76m	Mary Rand	GBR	1964
6.82m	Viorica Viscopoleanu	ROM	1968
6.84m	Heide Rosendahl	FRG	1970
6.92m	Angela Voigt	GDR	1976
6.99m	Sigrun Seigl	GDR	1976
7.07m	Vilma Bardauskiene	URS	1978
7.09m	Vilma Bardauskiene	URS	1978
7.15m	Anisoara Cusmir	ROM	1982
7.20m	Vali Ionescu	ROM	1982
7.21m	Anisoara Cusmir	ROM	1983
7.27m	Anisoara Cusmir	ROM	1983
7.43m	Anisoara Cusmir	ROM	1983
7.44m	Heike Drechsler	GDR	1985

Further Reading

BAAB publications
Adams, Gordon *How to teach the jumps* (1985)
Arnold, Malcolm *The Triple Jump* (1985)
Dick, Frank W. *The High Jump* (1980)
 Training Theory (1984)
Dick, Frank W., Johnson, Carl and Paish, Wilf *Strength Training for Athletes* (1978)
Kay, David *The Long Jump* (1976)
Neuff, Dr Alan *The Pole Vault* (1975)

The above can be obtained from:

BAAB/AAA Publications Sales Centre
5 Church Road
Great Bookham
Leatherhead
Surrey

Other publications
Dyson, G. H. G. *The Mechanics of Athletics* (Hodder and Stoughton, 1975)
Ganslen, Dr R. V. *Mechanics of the Pole Vault* (R. V. Ganslen, 1980)
Lear, John *Weight Lifting* (E. P. Publishing Ltd, 1980)
Payne, Howard and Rosemary *The Science of Track and Field Athletics* (Pelham Books, 1981)
Wilt, Fred *The Jumps – contemporary theory, technique and training* (Tafnews Press, 1972)

Rule books
IAAF rule book from:

IAAF
3 Hans Crescent
Knightsbridge
London
SW1X OLN

AAA handbook and Women's AAA rules from:

Francis House
Francis Street
London
SW1P 1DL

Index

Index

Crowood Sports Books

○ Also available in paperback

Further details of titles available or in preparation
can be obtained from the publishers.